CANADA

THE MEAT OF THE WORLD SANDWICH

Samy Appadurai

authorHOUSE®

AuthorHouse™
1663 Liberty Drive
Bloomington, IN 47403
www.authorhouse.com
Phone: 1-800-839-8640

First published by AuthorHouse 5/15/2009

ISBN: 978-1-4389-7926-7 (sc)
ISBN: 978-1-4389-7927-4 (hc)
ISBN: 978-1-4389-8937-2 (eb)

Library of Congress Control Number: 2009903931

Printed in the United States of America
Bloomington, Indiana

This book is printed on acid-free paper.

FORWARD

It was at a coffee shop in Toronto in 2007 that I first met the author, Samy Appadurai, who was interested in participating in elected politics in the upcoming provincial election. The author, who has the opportunity to reside in three continents and who indeed is a living product of globalization, has now made Canada his permanent home with his family. Canada is richer for his choice and the community benefits from his full commitment to the well being of our society.

As a proud Canadian, he outlines and explains the many characteristics of Canada as a nation, from his perspective as an immigrant. His experiences and those of other immigrants bring to this country customs and cultures that enhance, embellish and sometimes challenge the Canadian communities. The work is instructive and insightful while bringing particular issues to the readers attention concerning human rights and in particular rights of women who have immigrated from oppressive situations in other countries to understand and to appreciate the establish

The author, an experienced educator, outlines in some detail the importance of education or as he describes it as "investing in human capital". Canada needs to pursue an excellent educative system in order to maintain our economic and standard of living. With the mosaic of our cities and with many languages learned and spoken, teachers and students can benefit from the multicultural makeup of the classes

Canada's immigration policies have brought to Canada individuals and families from many different countries. With their energy and enthusiasm, many have found new opportunities, a safe haven and health care within a global village as they make their homes in the major cities of Canada.

Building the Canada nation with immigrants began long before Confederation. My own relatives came to Canada in 1825. The building of this great country continues. This manuscript provides a cursory overview of particular historic aspects of the early residents and some of the historical events in the establishment and building of our nation. With the two founding cultures of English and French in Canada, the presence of the American states forming a nation, and the further expansions of immigrants from numerous countries around the world coming to Canada, this book will be most interesting to grasp the essence of the Canada evolving to what it is to-day.

The many experiences that new Canadians bring to this country from their previous homeland are interesting and informative. The author himself enlightens the reader with his own personal experiences as an immigrant to Canada. Throughout the book the author demonstrates and reiterates his respect, care and love for others as he meets and greets other immigrants and citizens. He weaves a coherent account of life as an immigrant and the courageous life that he has experienced.

As a commitment to the country, in the best interests of the community and for the betterment of society, the author stepped forward to public life as a candidate for elected office. His example as an exemplary Canadian is a model for other immigrants and indeed all Canadians.

Ms.Pauline Browes

INTRODUCTION
TO THE AUTHOR

When first asked to write an introduction to draw you, gentle reader, to this written work? In an age where blogs rule and…. I paused to collect my thoughts as I considered many things. What would Face Book rants and ravings occupy too much of our intellectual free time; what would make this document different from the musings of, tens of thousands aspiring authors in hardcopy and virtually millions of anonymous habitués of the World Wide Web?

How would a book written in the traditional vein envisioned by compete with the electronic medium of this Age?

And the theme? Canada? A raucous, robust nation that has been analyzed countless times with the precision of a dentist's drill and – some would say -with similar disquietingly uneven results.

And finally, what of the author: Samy Appadurai? A refined and self effacing Canadian of Tamil origin to be sure, yet how could he draw and hold a reading audience in this, one of the most multi-culturally diverse nations in the world? What new voice would he bring to a choir that contains all the melodies of the global rainbow? What words could he possibly write, what images could he evoke – which would be unique or compelling?

But then I did what I am going to encourage you to do… I began to read.

And I continued reading for hour upon hour.

For this is not an ordinary omnibus, but a carefully thought, eminently readable book that bursts on the literary firmament like a Canada Day fireworks display- with effervescence and color and insight.

Samy Appadurai is a 21st century Renaissance Man and surely one of the most intriguing and compelling personalities it has been my pleasure to befriend in a lifetime spent living in three continents.

Radio raconteur, educator, global traveler, aspiring political candidate, concerned citizen of the World-- Samy Appadurai has experienced more in his fifty-some years on this planet than most would in a lifetime and he has done so with a vitality that speaks to a stellar brilliance of mind and clarity of thought.

In addition to his current role as a vibrant community leader in Canada, Samy has lived and taught in Africa; as the principal of a comprehensive secondary school in Ethiopia as well as in Nigeria and South East Asia in his homeland of Sri Lanka. He carries in his portfolio experience as an educator, religious counselor, newspaper columnist and radio talk show host.

This author's grasp of financial matters and macro economics is sublime. Intriguingly, he can, and does, write with the equal ease about macro economic trends as he does about the subtlety of the human condition under profound stress.

Samy Appadurai is eminently fair in his assessment, frank in his analysis and forgiving in his views-- be they concerning the fragile human condition or the Machiavellian world of finance as we find ourselves on the apparent precipice of what Charles Dickens would surely agree was "the best of times. and the worst of times."

Samy Appadurai's writing is a gem and this book is a crowning jewel in the intellectual heavens.

If ever there was a written work which I could and would commend to you as being incisive, entertaining and visionary… this is the one.

Read… and take great comfort in the fact that Samy Appadurai is optimistic about the human condition and human nature in all its guises.. And it shows.

Mr. CHUCK KONKEL

INTRODUCTION

While in the process of writing a book entitled "Canada- Center of the Global Nomads " a research book on global migration and emigration in relation to Canada , I was prompted by the press to write a series of articles on pressing Canadian issues. The appreciative comments and positive feedback on those articles by readers and friends motivated me to write more of them and because of this experience, this book came to be. The seeds were sown into the ground almost nine months ago and the harvest has yielded some great food for thought. I have named this dish "Canada – the Meat of the World Sandwich" and I hope it is a tasty and nutritious sandwich for lunch, if not dinner.

The approach of this book is based on various multi-dimensional experiences that I have had in my life; as a non Canadian citizen who viewed Canada like any other developed western nation, as a new immigrant to Canada with a wide range of experiences spanning almost two decades, as an expatriate educator in Africa from Asia, and finally as a patriotic Canadian participating in many social and political activities. In this book I share my direct experiences with facts that I have gathered along with wonderful thoughts from some very successful Canadians. My participation as a community activist, an author, public speaker, journalist and radio broadcaster along with the experience that I gained in politics has sharpened my thoughts and thus brought about this book.

I have been searching for a clear vision for our great nation of Canada and I know it is not an easy task but there is no harm in trying. This vision should provide a clear direction for the future and should include compromise in confrontations, attainable goals and promote patriotism along with providing a smooth transition of new immigrants from the total inclination of the ancestral land to their chosen new home country. Preserving and maintaining Canadian identity while having an unprejudiced relationship with the rest of the world, particularly with America, the evolution of the Canadian cultural mosaic, the declining natural increase in population and substitution by new immigrants, advocating for democracy and human rights, protecting the nation from terrorist activities, effective educational services as an investment for the future of Canada, cordial relationships between the provinces and the territories and the federal government , growing with the trend of globalization, and the direction of policy and basic philosophy of the government are issues that will lead the country and the people from the grass roots level to the crème of the crop.

I agree that global and local changes are inevitable and impact on the private and public life of individuals and the nation as a whole. This cannot not be ignored but the fundamental needs of every human being remain the same and each community or nation has defined the means of reaching their goals which have been shaped by their forefathers. This has to be respected, preserved and modified according to the changing times but, it must not deviate from the original plan. The philosophy is universal and goes beyond time and space but the vision of a nation or a community has its own boundaries and sense of direction. The Industrial Revolution brought a drastic change in Canadian life and the shift of the distribution of demographic patterns towards urbanization from the rural way of living but the Canadian way of living, thinking acting, and reacting has basically remained the same with some alteration, modification and integration.

My concern is that we have to maintain closeness amongst ourselves. In the cities, the settlements are closer and densely populated but the attachment from one community to the next is rather weak whereas attachments to the ancestral land remain very strong. I do not mean to say that we should ignore immigrant experiences or isolate them but we should extend our hands to other fellow Canadians and contribute equally to the production of the national cake. That way, we can all receive our due share and enjoy it together. This is not a new thought however it cannot be emphasized enough.

In this book I have touched many issues in a very contented fashion and the research that went into this book was delightful.

Samy Appadurai

ACKNOWLEDGEMENTS

I would like to take this opportunity to thank certain individuals who have given me their full support for this project. First of all however, I would like to thank them all for reading this book and providing constructive feedback. I would also like to thank them for their patience.

Special thanks go to The Honourable Pauline Browes of the Progressive Conservative Party of Canada. Pauline Browes has extensive government and public sector experience serving as a Member of Parliament, Cabinet Minster, Minister of State and as a Parliamentary Secretary. She is an adept in international government relations and serves on many boards and committees dealing with a variety of issues.

I would also like to thank Chuck Konkel, an accomplished novelist, entrepreneur, lecturer, political candidate and police officer who holds John A. Macdonald, Nelson Mandela and Sir Winston Churchill as role models. Chuck Konkel understands the power and potential of the human mind and works to instill a sense of pride in oneself and community.

I would like to thank Chuck for reading through my manuscript with an open mind for it is true that we live in an age where blogs and Facebook rule and one can find as many books about Canada as there are flavours of ice cream. I thank you for your kind suggestions and feedback along with your encouragement.

Special thanks also goes to Ken Kirupa an everlasting source of motivation. Ken, I thank you for helping me keep my eyes on the prize and seeing me through this project from start to finish.

Finally, I would like to thank you the readers, my fellow Canadians, for you are the inspiration behind this book. Without you and this wonderful country, this book would never have come to be. Thank you!

CONTENTS

CHAPTER ONE

MY CANADA

I was once asked to be the guest speaker at a Canada Day celebration in downtown Toronto, and readily obliged. Many new immigrants, along with their Canadian-born children, were in attendance.

While delivering my speech, I called on some members of the audience at random and asked them to make a few brief remarks on the significance of the occasion. Each person who spoke had something nice to say about his or her country of origin. Even those who had been born in Canada spoke glowingly about the homeland of their forefathers. I noticed a few Canadian flags being waved by little children, and many of those in attendance were wearing T-shirts that proclaimed them to be proud Canadians. This did not surprise me, but I was quite disappointed that none of the young people born in Canada said anything about living in this great country of ours. Indeed, none of the audience members who spoke said one word about Canada!

The interesting part of the background of these young people goes way beyond the Canada Day celebration. In the past, I had seen some of these teenagers carrying the flag of the nation of their ancestors and expressing their support of those countries when the World Cup matches, played elsewhere, drove much of the world into a frenzy of excitement. Indeed, at the time I wondered whether the heated competition and its reverberations around the globe might have added to global warming! I also wondered if such a match were to be played by a Canadian team against competitors of their ancestral heritage where these young people would stand and which flag they would wave. In the end, I could not come up with an answer.

The issue of ensuring loyalty is not a new phenomenon but is deeply rooted in Canadian soil. The Father of Confederation, the first Prime Minister of Canada, Sir John A. Macdonald, shared his love for Canada with that of his country of origin, Scotland. Sir John A., as he is affectionately known even today, was born in 1815 and was brought to Upper Canada (now Ontario) at the age of five. As an older teenager, he went back to Scotland, where he fell in love with his cousin, Isabella Clark. They soon married, and the young couple came to Canada in 1845 to build a new life. Although Sir John A. spent most of his life in this country and made many personal sacrifices in order to bring progress and prosperity to this land, he never lost his emotional tie to his country of origin.

Indeed, Macdonald was British to the core. Although he served as Canada's prime minister for 18 years, his loyalty to his ancestral homeland was profound. This is what he had to say on the subject: "As for myself, my course is clear. A British subject I was born; a British subject I will die. With my latest breath, I will oppose the 'veiled treason' which attempts by sordid means and mercenary proffers to lure our people from their allegiance."

When the 13 colonies in America revolted against the British Empire, at that point in time the sun had never before set on that empire. Those who fought for independence in the American Revolution were considered anathema by the British loyalists who chose to migrate to Canada rather than live in a land they considered treasonous to Mother England.

Although the Americans did away with the constitutional monarchy and became a republic, Canada continues to maintain the same system that remains in place in the United Kingdom, and the Queen of Britain is the Queen of Canada as well. I am deeply privileged and honoured to hold the Golden Jubilee Medal of her Majesty, Queen Elizabeth II.

The word "Canada" is derived from one or more of our native languages. In the Iroquois tongue, *kanata* means "town." In the Mohawk language, a town is called *nekanata*. Indeed, many other names were used to refer to this great country of ours before the name Canada was given, and the name of our country is said to have Spanish and Portuguese origins as well.

It is also reported that the first French settlers in this country demanded a "can a day" of beer; this is an interesting hypothesis of the origin of our country's name! Essentially, however, the consensus is that the First Nations use of the term Canada gave our country its name. On July 1, 1867, the British North America Act proclaimed Canada as the name of the new dominion.

Just as Sir John A. Macdonald was fiercely loyal to his roots although he led the new Dominion of Canada for so long, so, too, is William Jefferson Clinton, known by all and sundry as Bill, the former president of the United States of America. Although he was not reared on Irish soil, Bill Clinton has always had strong feelings for Ireland and, many years ago, did considerable research on his Irish roots. While in office, he made sure that everyone knew that he always celebrated the most famous of Irish festivals, St. Patrick's Day, and that he regularly received special guests from Ireland.

Heritage is a complex issue, and feathers are sometimes ruffled when people hold different views on the subject. Governor General Michaelle Jean recently paid a visit to France while Quebecers began their year-long celebration of the 400th anniversary of the establishment of the City of Quebec by Samuel de Champlain. In her speech, Madame Jean made mention, in a patriotic manner, of the significance of the event. It is more than a celebration of Quebecers, she declared; rather, the 400th anniversary of Quebec's founding is, as well, a celebration of all the descendants of the French who came to Canada's shores. Indeed, she said, more than a million of them currently reside in provinces other than Quebec.

The reaction to Madame Jean's comment by some members of the Bloc Quebecois was not encouraging, to put it mildly. Quite a few people were unhappy about her remarks. In this regard, it is noteworthy that when a former French president, Charles de Gaulle, visited Canada a few decades ago, he decided to promote the French heritage of our country in a very different way.

It is understandable that it is very hard to uproot the deeply held sentiments that many people feel for the place they were born. Sometimes I wonder where the hearts of those who hold dual citizenship truly lie. People who hold dual citizenships are truly people of two worlds—or more—as the intricacies of international law sometimes permit people to hold three or more citizenships simultaneously.

Though I am not a dual citizen, I have had the privilege of experiencing life on three different continents. I was born and brought up in Asia; I spent most of my middle years in Africa as a school principal and teacher. I have also made several trips to Europe, and have visited many places across North America. I have now had the good fortune of residing in Canada for more than two decades. Here I have been privileged to find a unique society that I have not seen anywhere else.

Officially, Canada is a multicultural, bilingual nation. It does not discourage new immigrants from pursuing their traditional activities; indeed, Canada supports multiculturalism. While expressions of prejudice and discrimination are seen here, they are relatively few and far between. As the great Montreal poet Irving Layton wrote, "We do not kill each other here as they do in the more civilized countries of the world."

Our government does not tolerate discrimination or the promotion of hatred in any form, and anyone who is a victim of such treatment has the right to report it to the authorities, who will take appropriate action.

Some friends who migrated to other parts of the world at around the same time as I came to Canada, recently visited my wife and me. While reiterating that we are incredibly fortunate to live here, they told us that what we have in this country cannot be bought for any price. Indeed, they remarked on what everyone living in the Greater Toronto Area already knows: In this city one can visit many parts of the world on the same day. There are Chinatowns both downtown and uptown, Little India on Gerrard Street, Sri Lankan enclaves in Scarborough and Markham, Korean communities at Bloor and Christie and Sheppard and Yonge, Italian and Portuguese neighbourhoods downtown, midtown and up north. Likewise, in many parts of British Colombia, Alberta and Quebec, it is easy to feel that one is not in Canada but abroad on account of the large pockets of immigrants from other places who have brought the best of their respective cultures with them to our shores.

Canada is the land of promise for everyone who migrates here. The foreign-born can become naturalized citizens, and such people face absolutely no restrictions in climbing to the very top of the ladder. Indeed, they can serve at the highest levels of government, which is not the case in most other countries in the world.

In this country, a person's talents, skills, education and experience speak louder than his socio-economic or ethnic background. There are countless stories of people who came to Canada as refugees, with little or no money, who worked hard and became millionaires. Some have even attained billionaire status.

Let us look at the backgrounds of Canada's current Governor General, Madame Michaele Jean, and her predecessor, Madame Adrienne Clarkson. Each of these outstanding women came to Canada as refugees (from Haiti and China respectively), and made significant contributions to our society before attaining this country's highest post. In the corporate and non-profit sectors, too, there are a great many successful people. While some socio-cultural barriers still exist, these barriers are not part of Canada's official policy; they are, in fact, officially frowned on.

I have heard from many immigrants of diverse ethnic origins that Canada has cultivated a very high level of tolerance. While the word "tolerance" is in popular use, I do not find it a particularly positive word. In place of the word "tolerance" I would use the word "acceptance." Acceptance reflects an appreciation of one another's cultures while tolerance implies a state of merely putting up with something. The overall acceptance of the mutuality and intrinsic worthiness of one another's cultures is a very positive force in Canadian life.

When it comes to Canadian foreign policy, we try to carry over our acceptance of others into the international sphere. Canada, a major world power located in the north, receives 80% of its revenues from export income. It would therefore be most unwise for us to antagonize our neighbour to the south and this, whether we like it or not, is our reality. Historically speaking, when Canada had very close ties with Great Britain, both economically and otherwise, it was, perhaps, less important for us to concern ourselves regarding how the United States felt about us or how the decisions taken in Washington affected us.

Nowadays the European Union has attained the level of a single economic bloc while the North American Free Trade Agreement (NAFTA) is not working out as well as its *signatores* (Canada, the United States and Mexico) had hoped. Both Democratic presidential candidates in the 2008 U.S. election have clearly indicated that they want to see some basic and drastic changes to the policy and framework of NAFTA. Fortunately, the United States depends on Canada for most of its natural gas and petroleum. (Until lately, the U.S. got most of its oil from Saudi Arabia. However, Canada has now surpassed the oil sheiks in supplying our southern neighbours.) Furthermore, the Hibernia Oil Sands, off the shores of Newfoundland, have become a gold mine of new opportunity for Canada in terms of oil reserves.

The major issue in terms of our foreign policy vis-à-vis the United States concerns the maintaining of sovereignty and the unique identity of Canada. Our legislated borders cannot be called into question, and we must be particularly vigilant regarding the protection and sovereignty of our Far North. Under no circumstances will Canada ever become the 51st state of the United States of America, as some cynics sarcastically comment.

In this regard, our government has increased Canada's presence in the Far North and assures us that our presence there will remain strong. The creation of the Territory of Nunavut in 1993 continues to strengthen the social fabric of the Far North while validating and promoting the flourishing Inuit culture that exists there.

With further reference to Canada's foreign policy, it is important to understand Canada's role in the British Commonwealth of Nations, the North American Treaty Alliance (NATO) and the United Nations (UN). In each of these institutions, Canada takes its own, independent stand. For example, Prime Minister Stephen Harper, at the recent Commonwealth meetings, condemned the undemocratic activities going on in Pakistan, and the flagrant human rights' violations being perpetrated in China and Sri Lanka.

It is particularly noteworthy that Canada always stands up for the rights of the poor and disenfranchised around the world. Our immigration policy is very generous, particularly with regard to refugee claimants. Canada has been honoured by various world bodies, including the United Nations, for its acceptance and treatment of those who have had to flee their country of origin on account of famine, natural disaster or armed conflict. The acceptance ratio compared with other Western countries is relatively high. Although most of the refugee-receiving countries base their acceptance or rejection of refugees on the Geneva Conventions of the United Nations, the yardstick by which the refugees are judged varies from country to country, to a certain degree. Some refugees, in fact, have been accepted by one country after having been rejected by another. This is one reason why many refugees have knocked and continue to knock at Canada's door from south of the border.

Let us turn now to the issue of Family-Class sponsorship. The reunification of family members of permanent residents and citizens of Canada holds high priority on account of the family values this nation holds dear.

Immigrants of the independent class make significant contributions to life in Canada. This group primarily encompasses skilled workers and investors. Canada is in need of qualitative and quantitative human capital for purely economic reasons, so immigrants of the economic class are encouraged to move here. Their contributions will help alleviate the shortage of workers caused by the expansion of the economy, the low natural increase of population and the high number of retiring baby boomers. In fact, economic-class immigrants account for more than half of total immigration. I applaud the decision of the Honourable Diane Finlay, Minister of Citizenship and Immigration Canada, for making significant changes in policy to reduce the backlog of applications for members of the potential independent class.

The following chart is most illuminating:

Permanent residents - Canada

year	Family class	%	Economic immigrants	%	Refu- gee s	%	Other	%	Catag not stated	%	Total	%
2006	70,506	28	138,257	54.9	32,492	12.9	10,382	4.1	120	0	251,649	100
1997	59,979	27.8	128,351	59.4	24,308	11.3	3,400	1.6	0	0	216,038	100

The number of new immigrants who were born outside Canada has reached almost 20% of the total population, a relatively high percentage. After a period of adjustment, most new immigrants participate fully in Canadian life and enjoy the many benefits it offers.

All in all, as virtually every newcomer will attest, Canada is the land of opportunity, not only for us, but for those who will come after us. Happy 141st birthday, Canada! Many happy returns to all Canadians and Canadian residents!

CHAPTER TWO

CANADIANISM CHALLENGED

In a previous essay, I quoted Sir John A. Macdonald: "As for myself, my course is clear. A British subject I was born; a British subject I will die." He made this statement in 1891 during the parliamentary election campaign while responding to the agenda of the Laurier Liberals, who were more inclined towards advocating for unrestricted trade and other extremely open relationships with the United States of America. Sir John A. in his declaration "A British subject…" was stating very clearly that he was a patriotic Canadian who simultaneously held himself faithful to the British crown. Under no circumstances would he allow the sovereignty of Canada to be tampered with. In his view, this involved not becoming too close with the foreign nation south of Canada's borders.

The truth is that Great Britain never wanted to interfere in Canada's affairs. People who left Britain for the New World on the same ship carried with them two opposing views as to what Canada's relationship with the mother country should be. As is well known, the process of establishing Canada's sovereignty was a complex one. Great Britain was grateful for Canada's unwavering loyalty throughout the American Revolution, and has never forgotten that support. The relationship between both countries has been very cordial.

Historically speaking, the Thirteen American Colonies, British subjects in other jurisdictions and the French living in Canada considered, for the most part, that their relationship with Britain was one of colonized subjects and their colonial ruler. As is also well known, many longed to slough off the yoke of colonial rule and struggled for their independence by revolutionary means. Many, of course, fought against the British Empire and won their freedom by the sword whereas Canada, from day one up to this hour, has maintained a mutually respectful and warm relationship with Great Britain. It should also be kept in mind that many British loyalists did not like the way the Thirteen Colonies treated Britain and instigated the revolution; the loyalists considered this gross ingratitude for everything Britain had done to support the colonies. The result, of course, was a totally broken relationship followed, with time, by an uneasy arm's-length relationship. Nowadays, thankfully, the relationship between the two countries is that of two sovereign states. After the September 11th 2001 terrorist attacks on New York and Washington and in the skies over the American northeast, the relationship between the two countries has become warmer than ever. The then British Prime Minister, Mr. Tony Blair, danced to the tune of the American piper President George W. Bush, until Blair's last day in office.

Canada as a nation was conceived a long time ago, and its delivery was normal; it was not a caesarian birth. The country's growth to nationhood was an evolutionary process, not a revolutionary one. While the colonies south of the border numbered thirteen when the revolution took place, the British North America Act of July 1, 1867, which, de facto, created Canada, was incorporated with only four jurisdictions: Upper and Lower Canada, Nova Scotia and New Brunswick. The Charlottetown, Prince Edward Island signing of the BNA Act gave birth to the wonderful independent nation we have today.

Historically speaking, Canada has been on its own path for a long time; it does not follow in the footsteps of any nation. Canada is sandwiched between the former and current great world powers—Great Britain and the United States, both politically and philosophically. This, many Canadians believe, is our country's greatest advantage and is at the foundation of our status as highly engaged world citizens whose work on the international stage is so significant.

Canada has another wonderful system that is an example for the whole world: universal health-care access. Mr. Jason Zengerle, an American, wrote in Mother Jones, "Most of us think of our neighbors to the north as living an American life, but perky Canada has many distinguishing characteristics: nationalized health care, fewer guns and more snow."

Last year, along with several Canadian friends, I headed south and spent my vacation at a holiday resort where there were people of many different nationalities. Interestingly, they judged us not by the way we dressed or by our "Canadian" accents; they judged us by observing the way we behaved. That was why they did not hesitate to ask "Are you Canadians?" In a very nice way, our reputation had preceded us.

Nevertheless, we asked them how they had guessed correctly. They replied, *"Canadians are modest, rational and respectful. We have noticed these qualities in you."* Instantly our red-and-white maple-leaf flag came to mind. At that moment all of us felt very proud, and our morale lifted. I am sure that the sentiments of those guests at the resort are echoed around the world, and this should make every Canadian very happy.

What is less known, perhaps, on the international scale, is that Canada is very generous when it comes to receiving new immigrants. This country has given its newcomers the liberty of openly retaining their love for the lands of their ancestors and has permitted them to morally support the cultures and institutions of their homelands while remaining committed Canadians. This is a mark of high respect for the backgrounds of others that is rarely seen in other countries. It is part of the great beauty of Canada that discrimination is not accepted here. According to official policy, one's country of origin, color, race or religion is irrelevant. The main thing is the way in which the newcomer behaves. Standards are set, and people are expected to meet them while being treated similarly to those of the Canadian mainstream and of those who have more recently made their homes here. Similarly, the education system of all the provinces and territories in Canada and their respective curricula leave no room for the odious practice of discrimination.

The warm welcome given to new immigrants in terms of their resettlement here has been recognized as one of the best in the developed nations. Canada's multicultural policy is special not only on paper, but in the daily lives of newcomers. People come to Canada from more than 170 different countries and from many different ethnic groups, and this country's cultural mosaic embraces all cultures equally. Up until recently, Great Britain, France, Italy and Germany have expected newcomers to conform to the mainstream culture, and their failure to do so has caused countless social problems. In these countries today, a more accommodative policy has been introduced.

People who support Canadianism can be viewed from several different approaches. Nationalists could be considered the first group. They are extremely cautious of Canada's relationships with outside world, the undue involvements of foreign influences on our affairs or the actions of certain governments, which they perceive as somewhat of a threat. They are particularly concerned about the actions of the United States of America, many of whose actions they consider interference to be stopped without any further delay. Such people are more or less inclined towards leftist thoughts like some politicians in the developing nations and the trade union movement in the developed nations. Even words like colonialism and imperialism are used by this camp. While their attitudes stem from patriotism, ideologically they have deviated from what is actually the case.

The second group is also patriotic but wants to be seen as not towing the American line. Brian Mulroney was accused by Jean Chretien of having done this. Indeed, it is very hard to draw a line and not cross it. The needs of the nation at any specific moment, the international situation, and the challenges facing our country determine what a strong government will do. The importance of Canada's current involvement in Afghanistan, in supporting the forces under the leadership of the USA, is well understood by the major political parties and majority of Canadians.

Our Right Honorable Prime Minister, Mr. Steven Harper, on August 19, 2008, in Hamilton, in replying to the comment made by a former Prime Minister, Jean Chretien, that he, Mr. Harper should have attended the opening ceremonies of the Olympics, as he, Chretien, attended when he was Prime Minister, stated, "I do not do what Bush does." This is an excellent example of Mr. Harper's standing up and giving voice to a profound sense of Canadianism.

Canadian's position has been overwhelmingly independent. We have not danced to the tune of any piper, only to our own music. Canada's tune has the rhythm of democracy, dignity, freedom of speech, freedom of the press and respect for fundamental human rights. As such, we share much with the American system of government. It is, therefore, normal that our country's ideology is inclined towards that of the United States, notwithstanding the reality that we disagree with certain aspects of American foreign policy. Many Canadians disagree, too, with certain aspects of American domestic policy, but what the Americans choose in that regard is beyond our sphere. Canada, for example, has continued to maintain its trade relationships and diplomatic ties with certain countries with which the USA does not. For example, Canada continues to have ties with Cuba, Iran and Iraq. America tried its best to establish an agreement that would allow it access to Canadian airspace for US missile defense on Canadian soil, and Canada flatly refused that request. The Americans are far from happy with that.

No respectable country in the world points its figure at Canada, even at this time when our national security is threatened. We are, of course, on the black list of certain terrorist organizations, not because of Canadian foreign policy per se, but because, in many aspects, we do support the agendas of the United States of America, which terrorists abhor.

According some politicians and academics, Canadian affairs are overly dominated, interfered with and influenced by the Americans. The Watkins Commission on Foreign Investment Review once stated that, "Canada is a satellite of the United States, the 51st state and the branch-plant economy. Canada 'should be master of its own destiny.'" I think that this statement goes way too far and is definitely out of line.

We should not diminish or denigrate our strong economic relationship with the USA, in that currently more than 80% of Canadian export services and goods are being bought by that country.

Canada has a very steady, reliable market south of the border, and there is no sane reason to give it up. In this regard, it should be noted that the European Union, the single most powerful economic bloc in the world, has partially closed its doors to international trade, preferring, naturally, to do as much business as possible with its own member states. China and India, which have become economic powerhouses, are now growing at respective annual rates of 10% and 8.4%. They are expanding their export base while lessening their import base, so while there is opportunity for Canada in those markets, it is not overwhelming by any means.

The slow economic growth of South American and African countries, with the exception of Brazil and South Africa, are not much help to Canada's bottom line. In fact, they need a lot of help from us. Whether we like it or not, we have to make additional moves towards helping them in terms of international aid and humanitarian relief. Taking all of the foregoing into account, then, it is wrong for anyone to consider us the undeclared 51st state of the American union. And, above all, our government, and, I must say, the American government, hold our sovereignty and separateness as special and inviolate able.

The former Prime Minister, Mr. Brian Mulroney, once stated, "Free trade with the United States is like sleeping with an elephant. It's terrific until the elephant twitches, and if the elephant rolls you are a dead man." This is an interesting comment, but cannot be considered entirely accurate. Despite the many drawbacks, NAFTA has had many positive effects on the Canadian economy.

There is no question of Canada's being pro-America. Meanwhile, Canada has not signed and will not sign any blank cheque payable to the USA. Nevertheless, a growing sense of continental unity will continue to develop among the USA, Canada and Mexico; this is a natural development as economic co-operation increases among the members of NAFTA, and, in this, Canada will be a very important player.

Anti-Americanism in Canada is not a new phenomenon. Ever since Canada has been a nation, that sentiment has existed. At times, advocating for Canadian sovereignty has meant, in certain circles, being anti-American. And, in those circles, if one is pro-American this has been interpreted as devaluing Canadian sovereignty. Nationalism is defined as love for one's country, not hatred or dislike of another country. Very tellingly, former Prime Minster John Diefenbaker once said, "I am not anti-American. But I am strongly pro-Canadian."

In my opinion, Canadianism is an ideology, a concept that serves to protect Canadian sovereignty. It is free from undue foreign domination in politics, culture, economic affairs or national unity. Simply put, Canada is not for sale.

CHAPTER THREE

THE EVER-GROWING CONCEPT OF GLOBALIZATION

Ms. Roberta Bondar, our beloved Canadian astronaut, flew on the NASA Space Shuttle Discovery in January 1992, for eight days, one hour and 44 minutes. While trying to locate our Earth from space, she must have felt overwhelmed, her vision changing to a new direction. When she was on Earth, like any of us, she likely felt tremendous pride in her family, her heritage and her Canadian values. Yet, when she stepped outside the bounds of our planet, Ms. Bondar must have felt even more like a world citizen. This type of thinking characterizes our idea of globalization.

Every fall, the birds of Siberia, Greenland and Iceland leave the northern hemisphere and fly thousands of kilometers south. In doing so, they cross the borders of many sovereign nations without passports or entry visas and they return when the warm spring air fills the skies. The fish in the ocean do not restrict their movements within certain boundaries; territorial designations mean nothing them. Even the thought of such things makes us smile; we consider them ridiculous. Nevertheless, a Canadian must fulfill certain requirements in order to travel to the USA, a fellow member of NAFTA (North American Free Trade Agreement). Isn't this just as ridiculous?

Today, even the man on the street can talk, at least superficially, about global warming, the depletion of the ozone layer or the smog caused by automobile emissions. How the world has changed!

The great natural disasters, particularly those of the past few years, have likewise brought the attention of the average person to the fact that we are all, indeed, citizens of the world. What hurts one often hurts many—or even all. The great tsunami that hit Asia a few years ago, with enormous loss of life, is one example. So is Hurricane Katrina, the tragedy that devastated New Orleans and its environs. The earthquake in Pakistan, the various genocides around the world that created millions of refugees, the drought in East Africa and the recent overwhelming tragedy of the earthquake Szechwan China are just a few examples. People everywhere stepped out of their comfort zones and opened up their wallets to help. They felt the suffering of their fellow human beings, and an outpouring of caring and concern followed. This is also an example of globalization.

Despite all the trade barriers, the breaking up of nations and the establishment of iron walls, the ideological conflicts and divisions, and the fanatical religious and ethnic wars, our world is becoming smaller and smaller.

The modern technological and information revolution is responsible for this. Today, even in the most remote, underdeveloped parts of the world, people have cell phones and internet access. Huge chunks of the middle class can afford to travel to previously undreamed of destinations. Money and commodities are traded internationally, often with a few key strokes, and multi-national corporations are found everywhere. Culture, too, has been greatly affected by the advances in technology and communication, whether people like it or not. Inexorably, across the globe people are coming closer and closer together as never before.

In the socio-political sphere, international organizations such as the United Nations and its subsidiaries, along with countless non-governmental organizations, are working together to solve important world issues that no single nation or bloc of nations can do alone. This, too, promotes globalization.

The industrialized nations are now co-operating to actively reduce global warming. These countries do not shoulder the burden in accordance with their responsibility for the current state of affairs. They simply put their shoulders to the wheel. Canada contributes far less to the damage being caused, whereas fast-growing countries like India and China still continue to use cheap sources of energy in a mass scale and pollute the air significantly. Nevertheless, these countries' contribution to cleaning up our planet is far less than their fair share. Generally speaking, the developing nations cannot afford the more expensive sources of energy at their current stage of development, so they continue to contribute to the negativity of the global environment. Their rural areas are quickly turning into urban areas, and demand for more energy is commensurate with this growth. Still, some of the developing nations are beginning to establish modern technological and industrial units using new equipment that will be less damaging to the environment. They have no choice if they, along with us, are to survive. If we do not take timely and aggressive protective methods to safeguard our world, in future 90% of the earth will be filled with ocean and the land mass will be reduced to 10% from the current level of 24%. Desertification will increase, and arable, habitable land will be reduced. Unless we do the right things now, as has been said so poetically in the past, there may be "water, water everywhere, but not a drop to drink."

In terms of political organization, some parts of the world are decentralizing while others are forming alliances. The Soviet Union has broken up; so has the former Yugoslavia. Many predict that the United States, India, Canada, Sri Lanka and other nations will split up into smaller units in the future. On the other hand, East and West Germany have reunited, and so have North and South Vietnam.

Where are we heading? Human societies across the globe have established very close contracts over the centuries, leading towards globalization. The seed was planted many millennia ago, and some of the waves date back 30,000 years, when North America's First Nations' peoples apparently migrated here from Asia via a northern land bridge that no longer exists. Later on, the Greeks, Egyptians, Babylonians, peoples of the Indus Valley and the Chinese began trade relations and set up other forms of international co-operation.

Colonization marked another wave in the globalization process. The Portuguese, Dutch, Spanish, British, French, Belgians, Germans and Italians colonized many areas around the world. Many "new" places were "discovered" by the European explorers. In addition to its negative aspects, colonization brought about uniform systems of government, education, taxation and trade, marking another stage in globalization. Indeed, it used to be said that when France caught cold, all of the French colonies throughout the world sneezed.

The Industrial Revolution in Great Britain was monumental in spreading globalization. It made work faster and easier, and greatly speeded up the rate of production, transportation and distribution. The Industrial Revolution also brought about dramatic social change. Machinery replaced a lot of unskilled labour, and, along with that, Great Britain was the first country to abolish slavery. The United States, Canada and other countries soon followed suit.

Then came World Wars One and Two, which divided most of the world into two opposing groups. The colonial powers forgot their rivalries and joined together to defeat Germany, Japan and Italy.

The between the former Soviet Union and the United States marked the following stage of globalization. Along with these two superpowers were a number of non-aligned nations that did not want to be under either of these two umbrellas. The Indian Prime Minister, Jawaharlal Nehru, did not create a powerful third bloc but did bring some of the neutral countries together on various levels.

As has already been mentioned, the current stage of globalization is marked by ever-growing advances in technology and communication. This process began in the 1980s and is intensifying every day.

The formation of the 27-member European Union is a prime example of what globalization can achieve. Originally aimed at becoming an economic union, far more wide-reaching changes have taken place. All member countries with the exception of Great Britain gave up their respective currencies and replaced it with the Euro. Then common immigration policies were put into effect. NAFTA, on the other hand, is experiencing some difficulties. Why is this so? Perhaps, in the case of the European Union, most of the countries have attained similar status on the economic playing field while Canada and the United States have done likewise; both are highly developed, industrialized nations. The third partner in NAFTA, Mexico, on the other hand, is still a developing nation, with all the problems that this entails. And, in addition, the two northern member states of NAFTA have been fearful and mistrustful not only of Mexico, but of each other. Therefore, they have established many protectionist policies.

A very sinister movement has also brought the world together against a common threat: international terrorism. Many former enemies have joined in a global effort to counter this unpredictable threat, and much more international cooperation will undoubtedly develop to beat this insidious enemy. The civilized world refuses to be victimized by terrorist thugs and will do its utmost to eradicate them.

In addition, population imbalances are rapidly making our world smaller. Many of the developing nations cannot feed, clothe or educate their populations, and there is a massive push for those affected, whenever possible, to leave for the developed world. Much of that world is unable to accept the unschooled masses; they are seeking skilled workers who can contribute to their industrialized economies. Therefore, refugees and would-be immigrants will do almost anything to be accepted into a First-World country. Meanwhile, the social climate of many such countries has been profoundly disrupted by the arrival of masses of people from the Third World.

The developed nations also want skilled immigrants to contribute to the growth of their respective economies as their birth rates continue to fall or remain stable. They are seeking those who have something to contribute, not those who will simply "take."

In addition, migrants from the Third World, whether educated or not, suffer culture shock when they arrive in First-World countries, and members of the mainstream culture often find these peoples' customs, beliefs and manners of dress extremely strange. It is very hard for newcomers to adapt, even in supportive societies like Canada. The second generation, however, adapts easily, which often leads to conflict between the parents who want to cling to traditional ways and the children who are being brought up in a different cultural milieu. This is particularly true in big cities where there are multi-racial populations and increasing intermarriages.

As we have seen then, globalization has penetrated everyone's life, directly or indirectly, and no stone will remain unturned. Globalization is a process, not an end. As we have also seen, globalization has its positive and negative aspects, only some of which we have touched on here. Nevertheless, effective communication and respect for our fellow human beings have the power to make globalization an overwhelmingly positive force. Right-thinking people want only the good for themselves, their families and, indeed, the whole world. As the world gets smaller, our interdependency will certainly bring us together as global citizens, not drive us further apart.

CHAPTER FOUR

VIOLATING WOMEN'S RIGHTS IS VIOLATING HUMAN RIGHTS

I recently spoke with a new immigrant, a woman in middle age. We met while I was visiting an English as a Second-Language program sponsored by Citizenship and Immigration Canada. This woman had been sponsored by her husband, but it was clear that she was uncomfortable here. Indeed, she appeared to be afraid of something. I got the impression that she felt that all eyes were upon her, and she watched people, and, indeed, the vehicles outside the window, in a very strange manner. I found this quite odd, as she was in a safe, public place where there were lots of people around.

After we had been talking for awhile, she broke down and told me about the agony and torture she was forced to endure behind closed doors. Her husband did not permit her to make a phone call to any man, even a relative. When she was out with her husband in public, even if a male she had never met happened to glance her way, she was subjected to cruel, inhumane treatment as soon as she got home. This included repeated beatings as well as emotional and verbal abuse.

Tragically, none of this was new to the poor woman. If, for example, she had any sort of appointment, even with a doctor or dentist, or any meeting in a government office, she had to recount to her husband every detail of what had transpired from the time she left the house until she returned. Indeed, she was like a private reporting to a commander, and felt humiliated every step of the way. For example, she had to give details as to how long she had had to wait for the bus, how long the bus took to travel each way, everything that had happened during the appointment, and so on.

If the husband discovered the slightest deviance from the original plan, the wife had to face the consequences. I responded to her pathetic story and advised her to call the police. Her spontaneous reply was "Don't you understand that I need to survive in my community?" By this she meant that if she complained to the authorities, she would have absolutely nowhere in her community to go for support and would be treated as an outcast. Now I am sure that there would have been somewhere for this woman to obtain some kind of support, but in her own eyes, she believed that this was not the case.

Men in these types of communities have all the social advantages. All too often, their masculinity means taking advantage of heritage values, degrading women and ignoring the laws of the land where they enjoy all sorts of privileges. Countless women from other parts of the Americas, Africa and Asia are now in Canada still enduring this treatment. Sometimes this suffering, because of their cultures of origin, continues into the second generation. Indeed, worldwide there are millions of women and girls who have been suffering because they have never thought to question the norms of their societies of origin insofar as the so-called "rights" of their husbands are concerned. Indeed, such women are treated worse than animals. It is instructive that, very recently, a Canadian court punished a man who had harmed his girlfriend's cat. Many of the poor women under discussion are treated far worse than that.

A typical case of gender discrimination can be seen in the case of Ms. Sofia Campos Guardado, who fled to the United States from El Salvador in 1984. While back home, she went to visit her uncle in another town to repay a debt owed by her father. Upon reaching her uncle's house, she found two strange men inside whose reasons for being there no one seemed aware of. These men had guns. They pulled her uncle, a male cousin, three female cousins and Campos into the back yard, then tortured the males and killed them. Then they let the female cousins and Ms. Campos go. They were told to run or be killed. In the end, one of them raped Ms. Campos. She and a cousin went to hospital, where they received treatment. After that Campos went to work in a nearby factory and chose not to return to live with her parents. Once she made a visit home, at which time her mother introduced two men as her cousins. She looked at them with utter astonishment and disgust, for one of them was the same man who had murdered her relatives and raped her at her uncle's home. The man then proceeded to threaten her and her entire family with death if she dared to reveal the rape. This prompted her to flee to the US for asylum.

Until very recently, despite pressure from international non-governmental organizations, particularly feminist groups, asylum seekers who wanted to enter Western countries on the basis of gender-based discrimination met with various challenges. Tragically, the international community did not realize the extent of the rampant woman abuse that exists worldwide, so they did not recognize demands for sanctuary as legitimate.

Even more tragically, persecution or oppressive, harmful or abusive treatment based on one's status as a woman was ignored and interpreted as part of cultural relativism. Canada, the first country to introduce gender-based persecution guidelines as grounds for seeking refugee status, passed this legislation in 1993. We were followed by the USA in 1995, and subsequently by Australia, the United Kingdom, South Africa, Norway, Sweden, Ireland and the Netherlands. In Canada, the working group on refugee claimants has been actively involved in the adjudications of the Immigration and Refugee Board since 1991. In fact, the guidelines established by Canada remain a model for gender-based asylum applications. In this regard, it should be noted that, in Canada, the Immigration and Refugee Board is independent from Citizenship and Immigration Canada, whereas in the United States the corresponding judicial bodies are tied to each other.

The revolution against gender-based human rights' violations has drawn the attention of researchers, feminists, educators, governments and international non-governmental organizations such as Human Rights' Watch, Amnesty International and the United Nations' High Commission for Refugees. Gay, lesbian and trans-gendered rights groups have also become part of the movement that is struggling for gender-based equality whether one agrees with their agendas or not.

The current definition of what constitutes a refugee is quite narrow, and this has caused many problems for those seeking asylum for alleged gender bias in their countries of origin. The current United Nations' definition of a refugee was established in 1951. It identifies a refugee as someone who, "by reason of well-founded fear of persecution for reasons of race, religion, nationality, membership in a particular social group, or political opinion,"

Right now, in most countries of the world, a woman seeking asylum exclusively on the grounds of gender bias would be conceptualized and treated as part of a social group, where the chances of getting full-scale recognition under current guidelines is rare. Under the universal refugee protocols of 1967, gender-based persecution is not recognized as an entirely valid criterion for granting asylum. Understandably, this is a very controversial, heated topic. The initiatives taken by Canada, the USA, Australia and other nations that have recognized it as being valid grounds for a refugee appeal. Hopefully other nations will follow suit. At the same time, there needs to be a change in the international definition of what constitutes abuse. Otherwise, the abuse will continue and intensify. The perpetrators must be made to understand that they are committing crimes against humanity, and that civilized people will no longer tolerate violence against 50% of the human race.

Women's inequality has been part of life for millennia. Discrimination and segregation have existed in many different forms all over the world. Issues of paternity and marriage, sexual freedom or the lack of it, issues of personal liberty, women's status in the workplace, in (or out of) politics, and, above all, in the home, have served to put women down and keep them down. Religion and culture have sometimes been used to devalue the status of women. As has been said, "Liberty is always taken; it is never given." This truth has been borne out over and over again.

In certain countries in the Middle East, in many parts of the African continent, and in certain parts of South Asia, particularly India, the law now prohibits, but, in reality, still allows, the practice of demanding a dowry as a vital element in marriage. Except in India, where the bride's family pays, in all other countries where this practice exists the man essentially "buys" the woman. On account of this, no relative of the bride, nor any member of society, for that matter, has the right to question how the woman is being treated because the man has "paid" for her.

In India, the problems faced by women are different. There, because the bride's family must pay the dowry to the groom and his family, any persecution she may face is sloughed off because, in economic terms, in many cases, the bride is considered a liability, not an asset. At the time of the wedding, if the promised dowry has not been paid in full and negative comments have been made, until the money is paid, the bride's life is truly in danger. In such an instance, the entire family of the groom, particularly the mother-in-law, tortures the bride by finding fault with whatever she does. They may treat her worse than a slave, to the point where she commits suicide.

To us in the West, that such situations exist is horrifying in the extreme.

The dowry situation notwithstanding, in many parts of the world women are always subordinate to men. The woman cannot ask for sex when she is in the mood for it, but whenever the man wants sex, whether the woman is prepared for it or not, she has to surrender like a slave. This is true whether she is sick or well; if her husband demands it, she is expected to deliver. Rape, forced sterilization and forced abortion are rampant, and women are always the victims.

Innumerable women have been persecuted under the system of polygamy, where the husband has the legal right to marry as many as wives he can afford, like King Solomon in ancient times. In fact, having many wives is a sign of a man's wealth and prestige. I have seen first hand the lives of women living in a polygamous system in Nigeria. One of my friends there was a businessman. He had shops in three towns and two cities, and, in each location, he had more than one wife. Altogether there were nine of them. Incredibly, he had a total of 43 children. Overall there were few problems because none of the wives and their respective children lived at the same location. However, in many cases where there are multiple wives, the wives and children live in the same compound in different rooms while the husband resides in the front of house, most often in a house like a palace. The senior wife has the power of directing and controlling the other wives. In the morning, for example, while having her coffee, she will give the directive to one or another of the wives to be with the husband, to give him all sorts of companionship and to sleep with him.

And, of course, by being forced to do this on account of her position, she, too, is being victimized and emotionally tortured, as are the other wives. The senior wife's beauty has, perhaps, faded over the years. She has to deal with other wives who refuse to obey her commands and with younger wives who flaunt their youth and their beauty, thereby putting her down. Sometimes the other wives band together to persecute the senior wife and her life becomes a living hell beyond the notice of the husband.

Some these victimized wives secretly take their children and move to another town, where they are forced to enter the netherworld of prostitution because they do not have the skills to earn a respectable livelihood. Then, for the rest of their miserable lives, they must endure the suffering of a prostitute. Nevertheless, many consider this preferable to their former lives as wives and chattels. This situation should be designated as a crime against humanity—nothing less—for that is what it is.

Such practices are abominable, and so is rape, which is widespread, especially in wartime. In Bosnia, for example, many innocent women were gang raped and many more shot dead. Rape is an act of violence that is often used as a weapon of war. By engaging in its horrors, men demonstrate their power over helpless women. Regrettably, on the international scene, rape is not considered serious enough a matter to justify it as grounds for seeking asylum. Political situations, of course, are considered sufficient grounds. Tragically, all too often rape is viewed as an interpersonal, non-political problem.

In male-dominant societies, females are oppressed and suppressed. The persecution of women is systemic, and is condoned by the social mores of the country. Therefore, it generally goes unnoticed. In most parts of Africa, it should be noted, calling a man a woman is one of the worst things one can do, for it shames the man and brings his manhood into disrepute. For example, when Milton Obote, the former president of Uganda, was attending a British Commonwealth of Nations summit abroad, Idi Amin engineered a coup d'etat, overthrew Obote's government and proclaimed himself president. At one point he defamed Obote as a woman. These kinds of references can also be found elsewhere on the world stage: On another occasion, a certain Israeli politician praised former the then Prime Minister, Golda Meier, as "the only man in the Israeli government."

Even today, multitudes of women and girls are undergoing torture, sexual assault, rape and forced marriage, which, as we stated before, the West tends to excuse on the basis of cultural relativism. Some women are victimized at the hands of sexual brutes that, remaining unpunished, spread waves of sexual terror among the population.

In some places, where true democracy is considered a weird and decadent system, all political power is concentrated within a small circle and the religious hierarchy has a direct and indirect hand in the political system. For example, in Iran gender-based discrimination is accepted as the law of the land. A man has the absolute right to divorce his wife. This concept is considered indisputable, but it does not apply equally to women. For instance, if a woman files for divorce and tries to get custody of her children, she most often loses that right. Furthermore, she is prohibited from entering certain professional and educational fields. Incredibly, in some countries the marriageable age for girls is as young as nine, and no woman has the right to marry a foreigner.

The power of high-ranking religious functionaries can be truly frightening and destructive. As soon as Ayatollah Ruhollah Khomeini returned to Iran after his exile in Paris, he declared that women could no longer engage in the teaching profession. And, with regard to his directive that women cover themselves up completely, he stated, on March 6, 1979, that "From now on, women have no right to be present in the government administration naked." He then proceeded to fire more than 40,000 women teachers, many of whom felt they had no choice but to become part of the crowd rather than socially unaccepted in order to survive. Segregation then became the law on buses, in classrooms and in sports activities. As was alluded to earlier in this article, the Geneva Conventions of 1949 did not include gender- based crimes on the list of crimes against humanity. Only the Rome Statute of1998 finally recognized gender-based persecution for the heinous crime that it is.

It is notable that, under the Rome Statute, a government in power that ignores, turns a blind eye or fails to protect a victim of gender-based persecution is considered an agent of that persecution. The governments of those countries where woman abuse is rampant must be bold enough to draw the line between age-old traditions that protect women against men who would violate their human rights. They must also educate the masses as to what is right and what is expected. They must attack this type of persecution vigorously, and the message has to emanate from the highest levels of government. The message should also state unequivocally that there will be zero tolerance for gender-based discrimination, and that those who perpetrate it will be prosecuted to the fullest extent of the law.

All of this must happen before more girls and women are forced into situations where they suffer and die en masse. This has very little, if anything, to do with true religion. It has to do with the notion of men being drunk with power over women and with using that power to emotionally and physically destroy them.

Even today, in some of the countries where I have lived, some ignorant, misguided people still believe in disgusting pagan practices. For example, when a royal or a noble passes away, he will still, even today, be buried along with a loyal subject—or even more than one. In such societies, so-called decent people forcibly kill those who are to be buried along with the distinguished person, believing that the murdered commoners will act as servants to him. This practice is eerily similar to that of the ancient Egyptians, who commonly killed people to serve their deceased kings in the next world. In our modern world, however, this type of murder can be viewed only as barbarism.

In discussing this, I want to point out that when there is a conflict between ancient cultural mores and human rights, now, in the 21st century, human rights must prevail. In this regard, I have heard stories of female babies being drowned in certain societies, and of so-called educated people excusing this practice, saying, "It's always been done this way." When will it all end?

Benevolent governments who are committed to the welfare of their people have a lot of hard work ahead of them. It is very difficult for them to challenge age-old practices because people's allegiances, built up over centuries or millennia, are deeply entrenched. This is particularly true when religious or deeply rooted cultural practices are questioned. For example, the circumcision of male children has been proved to be more hygienic than the lack of circumcision. Recent studies also indicate that circumcised males are less vulnerable to HIV and AIDS, as well as to other sexually transmitted diseases, than are uncircumcised males. Male circumcision is more or less mandatory for Jews and Muslims, for the Yorba ethnic group in Nigeria, and, in Ethiopia, for those who belong to the Amharic group. Female circumcision, on the other hand, has been labeled as a crime against humanity in that it does away with a major source of female sexual pleasure. Nonetheless, it continues to be practiced among certain religious and cultural groups worldwide, and countless religious authorities demand that it be continued. In those societies where the practice is ongoing, many "respectable men" will marry only circumcised women.

We should also keep in mind that some men also claim gender-based persecution at the hands of women, and that numerous men have been on the list of asylum seekers. There are, for example, recent cases in which female teachers and other professionals in positions of trust—most of whom are more than 40 years of age—have forced boys as young as 12 to have sex with them. And, as was mentioned earlier in this piece, gay and trans-gendered men, who consider themselves at great risk in their countries of origin, also regularly seek refugee status in more liberal countries.

The overwhelming statistics, however, indicate that women are almost always the victims of gender-based discrimination. The true numbers are hidden, as, it is estimated, most cases of woman abuse remain unreported. Most of these women suffer in silence as they are afraid of their husbands, their parents, their other relatives or the wrath of their respective societies. They live in frustration and fear, and pretend to be leading normal lives. Many are deformed by acid or by frequent beatings, and many are killed or commit suicide. Often they die young, after endless struggle.

Yet, despite all this, there exist many ways to hold back these abusive husbands. How can this be accomplished? By convincing governments in developing nations to pass laws that respect human dignity and enforce them. Education also plays a huge role, for many men; particularly in the developing world do not recognize the wrong-headedness of their abusive approach to women. The masses need to be educated, and government officials can no longer turn a blind eye. Advocacy for the rights of women has the power to lift millions out of degradation and despair, and, at the same time, reduce the applications of refugee status for alleged gender-based discrimination. However, for this to happen, the collective will must be there.

CHAPTER FIVE

EDUCATION: ARE WE DOING OUR BEST TO SERVE OUR CHILDREN?

I was recently honored to be asked to participate as a guest in a cultural event in Toronto along with Mr. Vincent Ananiathe, a vice-principal with the York Region District School Board. We were seated together in the front row and took the opportunity to introduce ourselves before the activities of the evening got under way.

Mr. Ananiathe and I have a lot in common in that we are both involved in education. I am currently the principal of a private secondary school and a former council member of the Ontario College of Teachers and he, as mentioned above, holds a high position in the educational system of York Region. We began to speak about various educational topics, particularly as they apply to the Province of Ontario. During our conversation, we got into a discussion about qualitative education, deteriorating moral values and civic responsibly.

I could not help thinking of Ms. Kim Campbell, the first female Prime Minister of Canada (and one who led our country for quite a short time). While attending election campaign meetings after the dissolution of parliament, Ms. Campbell visited a secondary school in Ontario, where she addressed the students. In the middle of her speech she spoke of the Quebec referendum. It appeared that at least some of those students, if not a fair number of them, did not have any clue as to what Ms. Campbell was talking about. This exceptional ignorance among the student body held an important message: it exhibited a profound lack of civic education in a senior segment of the student population, an ignorance that was virtually inexcusable.

The expectations and objectives of education from the point of view of many young people, when they think about it at all, sometimes do not tally with the aspirations of the provincial Ministry of Education or the ideas of their parents. All too often, young people think that education is primarily a means to an end, the end being equipped to take up a well-paying position. To them, money speaks more loudly than virtually anything else, and it does not matter whether the source of income comes from a white-collar or blue-collar job. Our young people today are living in the Free World, where they have a wide range of goods and services from which to choose, and, because of this great country of ours, they also have the freedom to do their utmost to possess these things as well. In this democratic country we call home, many new jobs have been created and the opportunity to find them is relatively easy when compared with most other countries of the world. For these and many other reasons, it appears that job-oriented learning all too often takes precedence over personal growth and development.

Unlike the Western nations, the situation in countries where there is authoritarianism, a dictatorship of the proletariat or other forms of oppression (where academic freedom is severely restricted), people have no choice but to follow the stereotypes and expectations of the societies in which they find themselves. All too often in these countries, people do not have the liberty or opportunity to create the lives they want. They live like frogs in a well.

Here in Canada, the doors of opportunity are open, although there are many people who, for social, emotional, cultural and health reasons, are unable to take advantage of them. Every day we read in the papers that taxpayers are worried about the growing expenditures made on behalf of education. Next to health care, the lion's share of the provincial budget goes to education. The major difference between the two is that, in the health-care sector, most of the money goes to expenditure. In the education sector, on the other hand, most of the money is invested in human capital. However, in the case of education, the investment does not yield an immediate output. Reaping the rewards takes a minimum of 12 years, when young people graduate. This is unlike the manufacturing industry where one compares input against output and then assesses the value obtained in monetary terms. As is not the case in other sectors, when it comes to education one cannot measure the overall outcome in terms of dollar value alone, as so many factors combine to produce an educated person. Nevertheless, the return from investment in education has to be assessed somehow and the necessary changes made when it appears that the system is falling short.

Old-fashioned parents tend to assess the success of education in very concrete ways. They look at their child's linguistic skills, focus on the accuracy of his grammar and spelling and look at his analytical skills in terms of mathematics and the hard sciences. As well, a child's problem-solving skills and the level of his moral outlook and behaviour are considered very important by such parents. Meanwhile, many parents today place more emphasis on the importance of their child's mastering the skills required by the technological and information age. That being said, today's educational system is trying to focus more and more on the overall development of the personality of every individual, regardless of his or her cultural or socio-economic background. Indeed, child- centered education is at core of what goes into the contemporary classroom. All children should have equal opportunities to succeed, and this principle is fundamental to our educational system.

It is important not to regard the term equal opportunity in a superficial manner. The children of mainstream Canadians, First Nations' peoples and visual minorities often do not perform to the same standard. Here equal opportunity does not necessarily mean the equal opportunity offered in our institutions of learning. Indeed, it goes significantly beyond the educational environment. Without question, the unbalanced socio-economic environment in which we live strongly affects young people's educational performance in academic settings. Are these differences genetic? I think not. Many factors contribute to the differences in academic achievement among the various groups. As has been said so often, one's economic background can be a criterion that influences academic success or the lack of it. Another is the cultural and social values that parents' ascribe to educational achievement, and this is based mainly on how they have been brought up.

Young people who come from low-income families where education is not highly valued generally have to endure poor living conditions. In some cases, for example, an entire family resides in a one-bedroom apartment and the living atmosphere is not conducive to intellectual, emotional or social development. Such children often suffer in other, less obvious ways. Due to a shortage of money, these children are not always fed a nutritious diet. As well, family breakdown is the cause of much suffering today. All-too-many children are being brought up in single-parent homes where the lone parent must work, often at a low-paying job, while trying to keep the children fed and clothed and keep a roof over their heads. In such homes, the exhausted parent is not in a position to give the children the level of care and affection they so desperately need.

The high cost of daycare is another factor that often prevents children from attaining their full potential. Poor working parents are often pressed to the wall and cannot find suitable child care, so, in desperation, they settle for substandard care. Countless research studies have proved that optimal child development occurs when infants, toddlers and pre-schoolers receive enriched education in their formative years. The well organized, well planned, properly supervised and properly evaluated activities of children by trained professionals in an early-learning centre contribute exponentially to the cognitive, linguistic, gross motor, fine motor and creative skills that lay the foundation for optimal child development.

Again and again it has been demonstrated that children who go through pre-school and nursery school do better in primary school than those who don't. In some cases, those skill gaps spoken of above remain forever, but, in the case of others, the gap disappears when sound education is delivered at the primary level. Habit formation begins during the very early stages, and, once formed, changes are very hard to make. Therefore, along with top quality childcare services, parents need a wide range of support to help them raise happy, healthy and well adjusted children.

With regard to the above, in all fairness, it is crucial to recognize that, in days gone by, things were different, especially within mainstream

Canadian culture. In those days, education began in the home, and many children entered kindergarten at the age of five with the ability to read. Who taught them the alphabet and early-reading skills? Most often the mother would be the one to do this. Alternatively, the father would teach them in the evening and on the weekend, when he was home from work.

In those days, education in and of itself was deeply valued, especially by the middle and upper classes, who considered it next to cleanliness and godliness, and its importance was instilled into children as soon as they were able to comprehend the notion. These days, on the other hand, it is often crucial that both parents work just to supply their family with the necessities of life, and there is often no time or energy for exhausted parents to communicate these values. As well, as mentioned earlier in this article, family breakdown has taken a tremendous toll in all sectors of our society. This makes the need for quality early-childhood education all the more important.

Unfortunately, the Ontario government has reduced funding for certain daycare services. Capital investment and operational expenses are insufficient, and subsidies for low-income families are not easy to get. This has put good quality daycare beyond the reach of many middle-class- as well as low-income earners. Even those households where two people are working often find it hard to pay.

In addition, declining school enrolment figures reflect the low rate of natural increase in the birth rate that characterizes this country. More than 10 Ontario schools have an overall enrollment of fewer than 10 students in a given academic year. One example is a tiny elementary school in the district of Caramat in Northern Ontario. Six elementary students used to be enrolled there. Last June, one of them was promoted to high school, and, next year, the total number of students enrolled will be reduced to five, unless new admissions fill up the vacancy, which appears doubtful. This is a reflection of the reality that exists nation-wide; it appears that declining enrollment has become the prevalent trend. In Ontario alone, 16 schools have a student population of 10 or fewer. Natural population growth has slowed over the past 30 years or so; historically speaking, school enrollment throughout Canada peaked in 1970-71 and declined thereafter.

Many people feel that the Ontario government does not adequately support education in this province. The recent cuts in Toronto's education system are a reflection of this, and the areas chosen to be cut are very controversial. Not long ago, the swimming facilities of many Toronto schools were closed and the closure of others slated. It has been openly stated that this is not due to decreased enrollment but is a result of the fiscal crisis affecting the school board.

While the budget for education, the sharing of responsibility for it and the allocation of resources to the various departments is clearly defined on paper, in reality there is considerable overlapping and inefficiency. It is alleged that, all too often, responsibility is shifted from the Ministry of Education to the district school boards. Then there is a tendency for each side to blame the other, and, amid the bickering, the problems remain unresolved. Both parents and children are sick and tried of this posturing, and it must end. This phenomenon is often seen when announcements concerning school closings are made; no one wants to accept responsibility or blame.

The former Ontario government of Premier Mike Harris attempted to curb expenses by reducing and amalgamating some of the school boards. People's response to this was mixed, and its effects are still being felt throughout the province. Harris's intention was to avoid the duplication of services that were costing taxpayers a lot of money, while the move was seen by school boards as a means of the government's taking revenge on them. Some people argue that services to children have suffered as a result of this initiative while others praise it as having been very cost-effective.

That being said, having smaller class sizes is seen as the wave of the future. Making this happen, along with better equipped classrooms, is one way to provide quality education. In addition, more emphasis needs to be placed on curriculum development, and in addressing the issues of disability of various kinds along with meeting the emotional and social needs of students. There should also be ongoing professional development for teachers, and they should be supplied with the most up-to-date instructional materials. Doing all of this will raise the standard of education.

Guidance and counseling, too, need to be addressed. Today's society is very complex, and students need to be equipped to face the challenges that life will inevitably throw at them. Young people need to be made aware that their actions have consequences, and that the choices they make will affect not only themselves, but their families, their communities and society as a whole. Our current educational and societal systems do not adequately prepare our youth for life, although the vast majority of people have the best of intentions insofar as educating the younger generation goes.

The complexity of our society requires constant, direct touch with our kids. In the multicultural stew that is the GTA, homogeneity no longer characterizes the student or general population. We are living in a heterogeneous society, where one man's food is considered another man's poison. In addition,

Globalization is becoming deeply rooted in our way of life, and its effects are far-reaching. Modern technology, too, has brought the world to our doorstep, and it is difficult for all but the most technically savvy to keep up with the rapid changes with which we are being bombarded. Indeed, these days anything that happens anywhere in the world can reach us spontaneously, and some young people regard any efforts to shield them from the realities of life as impinging on their notion of their right to uncontrollable wild freedom.

The school shapes much of what our children become. Students spend most of their time there, and the time they spend outside is often school-related. For them, homework and extra-curricular activities take up a good part of the day. The fact is that school and society go hand in hand. Anything that happens outside of school can not ignored by school authorities. They cannot say that a given matter has nothing to do with them and wash their hands of it. This is one of the many reasons why teaching is considered a noble profession, an elevated profession.

Many appreciate that our public-school system is open to all. Indeed, over two-thirds of children in Ontario attend public schools. Entrenched within the system, however, is the expectation that our schools will produce young people that are moral and behave ethically. Nevertheless, among all too many, the notions of cultivating proper values and believing in civic responsibility are not taken seriously enough. That is why, tragically, the police are now becoming involved in some schools on a regular basis. As far as I am concerned, this signifies a systemic failure on the part of our society. It is incumbent upon all of us to work together to overcome these challenges.

I have seen the curricula of different socialist counties. In many societies, free thinking is discouraged, and young people are lied to with regard to the value of the different economic systems. The glorification of dictators and authoritarian regimes characterizes those societies. In the schools in those countries, perhaps the only academic area where unbiased teaching is done is in technology. Nor, in such countries, do parents or their children have a voice in educational planning or in making suggestions that will shift the focus of education towards the notion of collective responsibility. In Canada, we are free to speak up for what we believe in and we are incredibly fortunate. Still, though, serious problems remain within our system.

Why, for example, is the school dropout rate more than a quarter of the total student population? This rate is particularly high among First Nations' students, who are followed by Black students and the children of some first-generation visible minority students. This is one reason why the Toronto District School Board has voted to establish some Afro-centric schools in the city next year. This undertaking has, deservedly, generated an incredible amount of controversy.

School dropouts contribute a great deal of negativity to our society. They lose their hope for a better future, and their dreams are shattered. They become dispirited and lose direction. Their adjustment mechanism finds fault with the structure of society as a whole, and they look at successful people as great cheaters who earn their wealth by illegal means. They do not respect the norms of society. Their frustration motivates them to get involved in various kinds of criminal behaviour. Once they have gone into jail and are returned to society, they know that respectable people look down at them; they know in their hearts that they are not truly accepted. This is one reason why many young people do not hesitate to re-offend.

Some of these disheartened young people create an underground world. They form gangs, and, having leaders to follow, accept the unwritten rules and regulations of membership. One of these principles holds that if any of them has not committed a crime but has been arrested, he should take responsibility for it—even if he knows that another member of his gang did it. He would never reveal that secret. This is part of a gang member's code of honour.

Gang members think and act differently from you and me. People are not born with criminal minds; it is circumstances that create them. Some factors contributing to anti-social behaviour include racial discrimination, lack of education, family background, poverty, social pressure, being influenced by unsavory elements, parental pressure, culture shock, generation gaps, and improper movies and television shows. There is something wrong somewhere and someone has to fix it. These serious issues cannot be left alone and passed on to the next generation.

At the core of teaching and learning is the expectation that the standard of education will rise to meet the challenges of our rapidly changing technological world. Yet, as we see all too often, this standard is on the verge of declining. In certain cases, I have seen expectations in the classroom lowered so that more people will pass. Lowered standards are a slap in the qualitative education. At the same time, I am in favour of standardized, provincial-wide tests. Their function, however, must be kept in perspective. One thing they do reveal is the efficacy of teaching the various core academic skills. These tests were developed in good faith and do expose the strengths and weakness of the schools through student scores.

In my view, all education in this country should be under an inter-provincial and inter-territorial umbrella authority. The 13 autonomous systems of education that currently exist should have a common ground and universal standards. This is something worth fighting for.

Knowledge, particularly technological knowledge, is universal. If we can accommodate the skilled workers who come from over 100 countries and allow them to join the labour market and become integrated within the Canadian system, why should inter-provincial differences exist in the delivery of education? The global village is upon us, and we must be prepared if we are not to fall behind. As well, international co-operation is upon us, and an excellent educational system is essential if we as a nation are to maintain our place as one of the world's most forward-looking countries. Space travel is at the forefront of international co-operation and collaboration these days; scientists and astronauts from several different countries, including Canada, regularly work together for the benefit of all.

While technological studies are very important, we must not underestimate the so-called soft skills that make us civilized human beings, and the funding cuts made to our educational system have cut these to the bone. Sports activities and all the arts have suffered in our schools. Where are the French clubs, the cooking clubs, the literary clubs and the debating societies of the past? They are hard to find in most schools these days. These co-curricular activities help develop good character, a healthy sense of self-esteem, critical- thinking skills, social skills, teamwork and leadership skills. Students who are involved in wholesome activities that interest them also have lower dropout rates and seldom engage in acts of racism. They smoke less than their peers, and tend to avoid the over-consumption of alcohol and illicit drugs. And, their names rarely, if ever, appear on court lists of juvenile delinquents. Likewise, such students seldom fall prey to teenage pregnancy. This is not a hypothesis; it has proved time and again to be true.

Today people's attention is focused on global warming, sky-rocketing gas prices and the exchange rate of the Canadian dollar versus other world currencies. Despite these and the many other challenges we face, we must put education at the forefront of our concerns and ensure that our young people are prepared for life, not only today, but tomorrow. Education cannot remain static; it is not a pool of stagnant water. It must be flexible and fluid, a river that is alive with energy and life, a river that is ever-changing.

CHAPTER SIX

LINGUISTIC LEADERSHIP

My years of experience being a program coordinator for the program Language Instruction for Newcomers to Canada (LINC) gave me the wonderful opportunity to interact with many immigrants from all over the world. Based on this experience, I became interested in the subject of language development and acquisition which prompted me to write this piece.

The acquisition of language is at the centre of overall human development and it reaches beyond the means of ordinary communication. Language penetrates into various other skills, such as research, analysis, discovery, invention, and the creation of new ideas, the exchange of emotion, sentiments, perception, conceptualization, abstraction. It is organic, a living entity that changes and grows according to time and place.

The Universal Declaration of Mandatory Learning states that children up to the age of 14 are to receive an education. The education of children is regarded as a right that is to be provided by the State. In the West, this provision is followed in both letter and spirit. However, this is not the case in many other countries due to factors such as: poverty, armed conflict, child labour, general ignorance and not knowing the value of an education. Canada is regarded as an educated and highly literate country, however among certain groups, the level of education and literacy is substantially lower.

In Canada, bilingualism manifests itself in many forms; we do not automatically think of French/English bilingualism only. We have different linguistic families represented in our many towns and cities most of them with very ancient roots. There are some crucial differences however. The English spoken by a person born and raised in a unilingual environment will be different than the English spoken by someone raised in a bilingual home. The same can be said for French. There is another situation where English and French are taught in environments where neither language is spoken commonly e.g. Japan, Germany, Korea. In this situation, the level of mastery and retention in either language is compromised due to the lack of practice and exposure. The bottom line is that we must master the host language and retain our ancestral language. The first allows us to integrate into our chosen country, the second allows us to maintain our connections with our cultural identity.

In Canada we officially recognize bilingualism in French and English, but in reality Canada embraces multilingualism. For example, on Dundas St. W and Spadina in Downtown Toronto, the street signs are written in both English and Chinese characters. On Pape Avenue and Danforth in the east end of Toronto, the signs are written in English and Greek. Though Quebec places an extra emphasis on the French language, in the various levels of government a multilingual approach is promoted.

There is a general worldwide trend in that there is a shift from unilingualism to multilingualism. This linguistic shift is more common in urban centres than rural areas. For example, many languages have their own numbering system like that of the old Roman culture and they are falling into disuse. But the Arabic numerical system has in many ways become universal and internationally accepted.

Modern technology has brought along a whole new language, sometimes referred to as the "sixth language". We can now "talk" to computers. Language is a system of communication and is a tool for conveying information. The ability to verbally communicate distinguishes us from other animals. Other animals are able to communicate with each other in a limited way using signals and signs. But the verbal communication of humans is unlimited, new words and phrases can be invented every day. The ways in which we combine words and sentences is infinite as any poet or creative writer will tell you. In the modern world, the usual definition of literacy includes not only the ability to read, write and perform simple mathematics but also includes computer literacy. Computer literacy and computer technology minimizes human contact and can solve the problem of human labour shortage mainly caused by the retirement of the so called" baby boomers".

In this fast paced world, the number of people joining the literate class is increasing due to the increased participation of the masses in civil society and a better quality of life. A higher standard of living can be achieved by being both being educated and literate. The modern economy has opened the gates of migration so wide that many can now move from place to place freely. This kind of interaction makes it essential to learn from one another.

There are 6 competencies in language acquisition namely speaking, listening, reading, writing, and thinking. Computer language is the sixth, but falls into a category of its own. The level of mastery in a language brings innovation in terms of invention and ideas.

There are many variations within bilingualism and multilingualism. For example there is a category known as balanced bilingualism in which both languages and their respective skills are used in roughly equal proportion. Another category is semi-lingualism, in which one language dominates over the other. Another sub-category within these 2 examples is academic/professional language versus the vernacular. When it comes to learning other languages, it is important to remember that with each language that we learn, the level of competency in each can be compromised to a certain extent. In other words the so called "richness" can be lost.

Socio-linguistic competency is also of great importance. Each language has its own culture if you will. For example an Englishman has a variety of language skills that are suited to his environment but his skills would not be suitable for the socio-linguistic environment of Greece. Each language carries its own social and cultural norms and it is important to learn these things. Merely speaking the words is not enough;

one has to know both the words and the song. You cannot separate the language from its roots, the roots carry the traditions, customs, culture and world view. One may go through a language, but the language might not necessarily penetrate into the core of your being.

Another important issue that faces many immigrants is the issue of professional language competency. For example, in Canada we expect immigrants to have a certain level in conversational English or French. But many immigrants from a professional background face a challenge in this regard. They are not conversationalists; they may be able to communicate well amongst their colleagues in their field, but not with the average person. In order to succeed, it is important to be competent in both levels of communication.

Ethno-linguistics is another interesting field which has a great influence. For example there are many countries in the world which have a spoken language, but no written script. There are also many dialects and accents within various languages. This can pose a particular barrier when it comes to learning English or French and also in terms of interacting within the greater society. For example, some languages have expressions and terms that are not easily translatable and thus pose a challenge for some language learners when it comes to creative writing. This can also make verbal communication difficult.

Let us now look into the second and third generation of non English or French speaking immigrants to Canada. As far as my research into heritage language study by 20 different ethnic groups shows, only 30% or less are effectively learning these languages. In most cases, they are functionally literate but they learn English or French in Canada as their first language. There is a big difference in learning a language as ones mother tongue versus as a first language. By mother tongue I am referring to not only the language but also the socio-linguistic norms associated with it. In the modern world where technology dominates every aspect of our public and private life, except for high research intellectuals for an average or semi skilled person, the command of linguistics has been swallowed by technology. The need for linguistic mastery has been diluted.

In the evolution of languages, some languages die out and some are born. In South Africa among the European settlers, the Dutch, German and the English speaking immigrants intermingled and produced a language known as Afrikaans. Hebrew, one of the oldest languages in the world was not spoken by the common people and reached the stage of what we refer to as a "dead" language and has been revived only recently. When 2 equal languages intermingle both of them will survive. When a language dominates another, the weaker one will eventually fall into disuse. Some so called "dead languages" are still used by some segments of various cultures. For example, Pali the language spoken by the Buddha, though it is not spoken by common people today is still used in the ceremonial chanting and prayers performed by Buddhist monks in Southeast Asia. The same can be said for the use of Latin in the Vatican.

There are many languages on the brink of extinction. In a number of countries there are only a handful of speakers and when they die, the language dies with them. For example many First Nations languages suffered this fate after European contact. Sometimes the socio-cultural norms prevent the language from surviving. For example in Australia, there is a cultural taboo that prevents siblings from speaking to each other in certain Aboriginal languages. Research into language survival says that there are over 6000 languages spoken in the world today; within a century only 10% of them will survive. This is very frightening, for when a language dies, so does the culture and the history.

The third generation of many new immigrants will be illiterate in their heritage language. It is unavoidable and whatever steps we take to preserve these languages will not yield significant results. Therefore whether we like it or not we have to accept the reality that is the command of a language beyond just the basic competencies, and for Canadians it should be either English or French. It does not mean we should not advocate for the retention of our heritage languages but rather shift our focus to the language of our chosen country.

Most of the new immigrants at the initial stage or longer confine themselves to a minority language spoken environment within a majority language spoken area. It becomes a kind of language community. There will be a constant change between the minority and majority languages and certainly the majority language will supersede the minority. The minority language will be spoken mainly in the home and in certain cultural circumstances, such in ones place of worship. So the chances of developing and practicing the minority language are limited. These minority languages are spoken in an informal manner within the family whereas the majority language is used in a more formal context. This situation arises within immigrant communities that are of neither British nor French in origin. For example, in the city of Toronto over 165 languages are spoken. When the majority language is used as the medium of instruction, the language of business and the language of daily life, the minority language falls into disuse and is replaced by the majority language.

For example, using historical Canadian immigration patterns, the Ukrainian communities that settled in Western Canada were more able to preserve both their original written and spoken language. Whereas in the urban centers such as Toronto, Montreal and Vancouver, the use of minority languages by new immigrants became limited and the majority language, in this case being English was adopted. The periodic influx of new immigrants into the urban centers ensures the continuation of minority language use as these new immigrants take time to integrate into the mainstream culture.

There is an interesting case however when it comes to learning the majority language. Undocumented immigrants, some of whom are smuggled into the country are deliberately prevented from learning the majority language in order the keep them in subjection.

There is a misconception held by many people that learning and using 2 different languages with children is a burden on the brain and can lead to confusion. This is not the case at all. In fact there is demonstrable proof that children who use 2 different languages often have better linguistic, creative and social skills than monolingual children. It is also said that bilingualism leads to more brain elasticity and each language becomes compartmentalized within the brain as evidenced by MRI scans performed on bilinguals. It is quite fascinating to see how the brain stores language and this is proof that one does not become confused when learning 2 or more languages. In terms of social interaction people who are bilingual have better listening skills and can respond more appropriately in social situations.

However, bilingualism has not always been held with such high esteem. We can find many historical examples of what one could call "language murder". For example, in Guyana, though the majority population was originally laborers of East Indian descent, the use of Hindi was forbidden by the British and now a language that is a mixture of Hindi and English remains which is spoken only by people of a certain age. In Canada, many First Nations languages were wiped out as a result of the Residential School system. Children were severely punished for speaking in their original language until eventually there remained until recent times, only a handful of speakers. This injustice is being remedied however. Many First Nations communities are relearning their languages and are teaching them to their young people.

In actual fact there is no multilingualism, there is only ones first language and the rest of the languages the person may speak be it two, three or more. The skills acquired from learning ones first language are transferable with each additional language. These skills are likewise, not a burden on the brain and do not cause any hardship but can in fact enrich ones thinking and worldview. One example is the word "Ysgol" in Welsh which means both "ladder" and "school". Thus a Welsh speaking child who also speaks English would come to think of school as a ladder metaphorically speaking.

In this age of globalization, it is not feasible for a person to be monolingual if one is going to survive. It is important to learn more than one language. On the other hand the development of technology is posing a particular challenge in this regard. Technical skills are replacing language skills at an increasing rate; one does not need to speak much when operating computer equipment. In conclusion we must all be concerned about the linguistic development of our young people for language is power.

CHAPTER SEVEN

NEW IMMIGRANTS BRING NEW BLOOD AND NEW ENERGY TO CANADA

I had just spent my vacation in a sub-tropical paradise and returned to Toronto's freezing weather. Even more than the warm welcome my family gave me, a pile of bills welcomed me with the additional expectation of a spontaneous response. The accumulated bills scared me because my holiday expenses had gone way beyond my budget. I had to tighten my belt. I paid all the bills and was left with just a few dollars with which to go shopping. So, I made my way to a well-known store where things are truly inexpensive. As I was leaving at closing time, one of the employees, who had finished her work for the day, was kind enough to help me carry my purchases to the car. In return I offered to drop her off at her home which, she had mentioned, was not far from mine.

While we were chatting, I noticed a wave of anxiety and disappointment on her face. I was aware that the lady was a new immigrant to Canada. I asked her, "How long you have been in this country?" She told me she had arrived two years ago, under the independent class provision, in the skilled worker category. She further told me that she had been a doctor and her husband an engineer in their country of origin.

I knew that most skilled newcomers, like this lady, had completed post-secondary education of some kind and that a large percentage of them were highly qualified professionals. In their home countries they had held high, responsible positions, and had enjoyed many long years of success, along with its accompanying high status. Simply put, back home they were the cream of the crop, and I could see that the lady I was driving was a highly refined and educated individual.

I have met several such people in Toronto. Their overall expectations have not been realized, and the truth is that their life in Canada, at its initial stage, is a very bitter pill to swallow. Highly skilled immigrants arrive on our shores full of sweet dreams that they will fit easily to our system and that a better life will be theirs almost instantly. Unfortunately, however, when they turn on the tap, it is only well treated, healthy and fresh water that flows out, not milk and honey. (That being said, to many, the sweet, fresh water is a blessing they never had back home, and they are most grateful for it.)

I told the lady about the experiences of those like her whom I have been privileged to meet. In Canada, I told her, it is a miniature world where immigrants and refugees from more than 170 countries have come together, with their many talents, to further build up our great nation. When she expressed her frustration at not having her qualifications recognized, I told her: If Canada directly accommodates every immigrant in his or her field of specialization without having uniformity in terms of recognizing their training their professional qualifications will be of an uncertain quality, and disaster—social, professional and economic—will follow. Therefore, I said, for the best interest of the nation and for the newcomers, the hardships they face not withstanding, a certain amount of training and updating of qualifications, to assure professional excellence and uniformity, are essential. Even though I sympathized with her, I said that there should be no exceptions to this policy.

As my car reached this lady's apartment building and we said our good-byes, I encouraged her as best I could to follow her dream of qualifying to work as a doctor here. I will not forget this lady, who is willing to do work way below her professional level to gain a foothold in Toronto with the vision of practicing her true profession later on. She is a fine example to other new immigrants, and, indeed, to us all.

Migration, of course, is not a new phenomenon. From very early on, people did not stay in one place, but were, in fact, wanderers. It is now widely accepted that Canada's First Nations' peoples, too, migrated here from Mongolia in pre-historic times across a land bridge that no longer exists. Archaeological findings indicate that, even after arriving on these shores, they migrated from place to place. Only after they began to cultivate the land did they begin to establish settlements.

Subsequent global migration has been caused by continental drift, climate change, and by natural calamities such as drought, flood, volcanic eruption and tidal-wave. Man-made factors have also contributed to mass migration: war, trade, exploration, and colonization, among many other factors. In today's global village, migration on a large scale is inevitable.

From a historical perspective, those who have populated this country, along with their descendants, can be categorized into twelve separate groups: (1) First Nations' peoples (who, as stated above, are thought to have come to Canada from northern Asia) (2) slaves (3) indentured servants (4) traders (5) warriors (6) contract workers (7) refugees (8) through marriage (9) skilled workers (10) investors (11) those born here and (12) family-class sponsorship.

The international growth of human resources and the means of their distribution are undergoing a period of dramatic change. In many instances, migration is linked with economic disparity and population imbalance. Population growth in most of the developed world remains stable or is declining, while, in the developing world, the population continues to grow. That being said, certain governments, such as that in Uganda, where the birth rate is very high, have introduced initiatives to help slow population growth. China's one-child policy is likewise an attempt to control the numbers of people being born there, and is a statistical, if not social, success.

Overall, the world's population continues to increase rapidly, while people's needs have, more and more, become the focal point of policy making on the part of governments and their handmaidens, the economists and statisticians. For the first time in the history of the world, particularly in those countries that are democracies, every individual, irrespective of his social status, education, race, religion, economic strength or other social norms, is highly valued and respected—in principle, if not always in practice.

The effects of the Industrial Revolution that took place in Great Britain a couple of centuries ago reverberated all around the world. Indeed, the technological advancement that followed in its wake began the journey towards the development of the global village that exists today. Industrialized economies turned national, closed economies became wide open and paved the way for greater individual and social interdependency, especially in economic terms, than had ever been known before. No country in the world today—whether a market economy or a centrally planned economy—could exist in a vacuum without interacting with the rest of the world.

Largely on account of this international connectivity, the demand and supply for human resources has been shifting geographically and growing exponentially in First World and Second World countries. Supply is based on an increase in population and the local demand for outstanding human capital to fill the need.

In this regard, it is interesting to note that population growth has four main stages. In the first stage, in less developed countries, the inferior development of the economic and other sectors contributes to high birth rates and infant mortality. In the absence of a developed manufacturing sector, agriculture and trade are the mainstays of the economy. In such economies, no significant industrial framework exists to hire significant numbers of workers.

In the second stage, higher standards of living, mass education and improved health facilities cause the death rate to decline faster than the birth rate. As a result, the gap between the two becomes wider. It is predicted that, within the next twenty years, the population of India will outstrip that of China. Meanwhile, Canada's birth and death rates remain relatively equal, although both have declined significantly in recent years.

In Canada today—indeed, everywhere, in principle if not in fact—children should not be considered liabilities; they are our resources of tomorrow. They are certainly dependents now, and the tax system necessarily devotes a high percentage of a nation's wealth to them. As stated, a great deal of the money and other resources we devote to children is an investment. Nevertheless, it is very hard for a developing nation to invest as much money as is needed in children's health and education; therefore, in many of those places, children do have access to adequate medical care and education. It is interesting to note that, in Canada, the decline in the birth rate has reduced our current investment in children, and that this has had negative connotations in terms of our economy.

On the other hand, the so called baby-boomers now account for more than twelve per cent of Canada's population. This number is unusually high for a specific age cohort. As the baby-boomers retire, they, too, as senior citizens, become dependants of a different sort. Whether we like it or not, our increasing expenditure on seniors is the moral obligation of every society.

In the third stage, the standard of living has improved drastically. Many things that were once considered luxuries have become essentials. The desire for a good education is now viewed, by most people in Canada, as a need, not a "want." Whether or not to educate one's children is not longer an option. Child labour, of course, is illegal here. Education is considered a basic right of a child, and providing it is the responsibility of the state. Yet, on account of the exponential rise in the cost of living, providing children with what they need has become incredibly expensive. As well, modernization has brought about many avenues for entertainment, a concept that holds little or no value in most of the Third World. The very concept of entertainment is foreign to millions of people globally while it is taken for granted here.

At the fourth stage, both the birth rate and death rate slow down. At the latter part of this stage, at some point the death rate supersedes the birth rate, and several industrialized countries are moving towards this. If Canada were to close its doors to immigrants, in approximately two hundred years not a single person would be living in this country.

Clearly, Canada has entered the early part of the last stage. This country can no longer depend solely on natural population growth on the part of those who live here now. Whether one likes it or not,

Canada needs a constant influx of new immigrants both to keep up the birth rate and to ensure this country's economic growth.

During the last election, our Prime Minister, the Right Honourable Stephen Harper, insisted that there be increased protection of our northern border. Before he brought this issue to light, many Canadians did not realize its importance. However, when Russia and the United States began to focus on the oil, diamonds and other minerals in the Far North, we came to see the need for the defense of our northern regions and for maintaining the integrity of our sovereignty there. Thank you, Mr. Prime Minister, for bringing this matter forth as an issue of great public concern.

In view of the increasing importance of the Canada's Far North and the need for skilled labour all across our nation, we need more skilled workers in this region. As was noted earlier, Canada's present birth rate does not produce enough people to do all the work that needs to be done, the improvements in technology notwithstanding. We need a constant flow of immigrants. Here the question arises: Who gets the most benefit, the sending country or the receiving country? Sending countries invest heavily in their people, but before they can recoup this investment, their people leave. On the other hand, the receiving country reaps the benefits of the investment of the sending country without much, if any, investment. Most newcomers to Canada, it should be noted, are between the ages of twenty-five and forty-five, and are highly skilled.

Are these immigrants invited here for purely economic reasons, or are there other reasons as well? Many factors are involved when it comes to deciding whom Canada will accept. As is well known, the reunification of families is considered a priority here for humanitarian reasons. As is also well known, Canada's multicultural policy remains in full force. Indeed, it can be said that Canada's immigration policy is multi-dimensional.

In the era of the early European settlers, around five hundred years ago, the door was open mainly to the British and the French. They settled, of course, primarily in what is now Ontario and Quebec, although settlement in Newfoundland and the Maritime Provinces began around the same time. Most of Canada west of Ontario was virgin land, and more people were needed to settle the western regions and convert the forests into arable land. Eventually the decline in migration from Britain and France led to a need for immigrants from other places, and at this time the immigration door was opened to those from Eastern and Southern Europe. This is how Canada's west was built.

The influx or slowdown of the arrival of newcomers is determined by two opposite forces—push and pull forces. Whenever there is a famine, a population explosion, a natural calamity, armed conflict and so on in the sending country, the push force will send more migrants to other parts of the world. At the same time, when the receiving country is economically strong, with a high standard of living and offering great opportunity for education and employment, those are considered pull factors. These, coupled with a slowdown in the natural growth of population and a high demand for manpower, pull many migrants from Third World to First World countries. Quite often, both push and pull factors are at work.

In addition to the reasons discussed above, other issues also contribute to the push/pull factors that come into play. Governmental policies, issues pertaining to cultural preservation, ethnic tensions, language, religion, etc., all have a profound influence as to whether people leave or stay in their home countries.

Canadian's immigration policy has been carefully designed. At specific times in the past the government was concerned that Canadian values should not be tampered with or altered by the arrival of a large number of people from specific ethnic or religious groups. At other times governmental policies towards new immigrants may have been superficially warm, but there was sometimes a hidden agenda behind bringing them here.

Canada's immigration policy before 1978 was explicitly biased against Asians and other minorities. For example, the Canadian Immigration Act of 1910 expressed an overt bias against certain groups, and it empowered Cabinet to prohibit the admission of immigrants on racial grounds. Although the wording of the Act was changed several times, its provisions remained intact until 1978. In fact, in 1919, Cabinet had the power to bar from Canada any immigrant from any race on the grounds that members of a given race were undesirable. Part of the Act read as follows:

"Owing to their peculiar customs, habits modes of life and methods of holding property, and because of their probable inability to become readily assimilated…"

The Act affected Germans, Austrians, Hungarians and Bulgarians by the Order in Council of March 14, 1919. Asians, too, were denied free entry into Canada from 1923 until 1956, with the exception of farm laborers, domestic workers and spouses of Canadian citizens. A Head Tax was levied on Chinese immigrants. Under the Chinese Immigration Act of 1885, Chinese who wished to settle in Canada had to pay a Head Tax of $50. In 1900 this was increased to $100, and, in 1903, it was again raised to the huge sum of $500. Great honour and respect goes to our Prime Minister, the Right Honourable Stephen Harper, for apologizing for the Head Tax imposed by his long-ago predecessors and for extending compensation to those affected by this racist policy.

The Immigration Act of 1978 brought true democracy to Canada's immigration process and removed the discrimination inherent in the previous Act. Today's Canada is a role model and an example for the entire world. Canada is the only country that accepts newcomers regardless of whether they are from the independent class, family class, sponsored class or refugees; all are received in the same manner. Canada extends its hand to eligible newcomers with a broad smile and a warm welcoming package. On the other hand, many other countries are hesitant to accept refugees, as defined by the Geneva Convention, and take them in only with the proviso that they will return to their home countries once the situation improves there. In certain countries, even refugees' children and grandchildren who were born in the country are not granted citizenship.

As we have seen, therefore, Canada is a country built by immigrants and refugees. Their contribution to our economy and our cultural and social life has proved invaluable. All of us are the richer for their presence. New Immigrants bring new blood and new energy to Canada.

CHAPTER EIGHT

NEW IMMIGRANTS ARE OUR ASSETS

It was a pleasant morning, at about 7.30 a.m. on a working day; I drove my car to the Kennedy subway from my home in Scarborough. There was free parking in the subway parking lot for people who hold the monthly Metropass. I preferred to travel by the public transportation, due to the only reason that I could make use of the traveling time without any interruption from cell phone calls. A major portion of my book entitled "*The Global Nomad in Canada* " and this whole article was written on the train. I parked my car and got into the subway station at about 8 a.m. Since it was the peak of the morning rush hour I saw many passengers hurrying to catch the earliest train. Some of them though late for work, rushed to the paper stand and grabbed a copy of the *Metro*, a free paper while walking down to the platform. It looked like a miniature world.

It was really an amazing scene. There was nothing unusual happening on that very day. It was one of those typical working days. I could see most of them dressed up in an urban Canadian fashion. But I began to see their long rooted backgrounds beyond their outer appearances. I was wondering about their entire background. Where have they come from; what kind of languages they speak; what kind of faith they have; what form of their cultural and social values exist within themselves; what kind of food they eat and so on. How do they share the Canadian values with their uprooted heritage values. My mind also turned to the "Canada first' moment that was formed by some patriotic Canadians just a year after the confederation on 1ˢᵗ July 1867. Eventually the moment died, but the concept survives underneath the grass.

Immigrants have certain qualities in common and it will continue with small or no alterations. Some of them are new to the urban cultures; some are new to the non urban Canadians too. The revolution of technology has brought some impact on lifestyle. If these new immigrants would have returned to their country of origin they might have noticed the changes.

The distribution of the age in new immigrants does not go parallel to the natural distribution of the population in many ways... In the developing countries the bulk of population is in the age group of below 20 years of age. It goes slightly alerted on the bell shape. The bell shape is considered as the normal pattern of the age distribution of population. In that shape the youth and the seniors are too low in percentage and bulk of the population in the middle age. But right now in the Canadian population the seniors account for almost 13% it is slightly higher than then the normal pattern. The reason for it the baby boomers that were born just after the Second World War in 1945 onwards turned into seniors.

A large portion of the new Immigrants irrespective of their country of origin and the category, the early middle-aged ones are more in number than the bell shaped curve. The number of children in both groups is low. Among Canadians the slow down in birth rate and among new Immigrants the children would not be able to take an adventure trip by themselves. They have to be accompanied by the older ones. The older ones could bear the hardship in their country, usually do not prefer to be uprooted, unless and otherwise the political and economic condition is extremely pressing. They are very much accustomed to their environment where they were born and brought up. The people who had positions, well to do and leading a successful life normal remain in their land and whenever they face hardship they consider it as a passing clouds.

It reminds me an interesting incident that happened to my friend who had been working as Doctor at the district of Ado-Ekit, Ondo state, Nigeria. He had a medical assistant in the health clinic. My friend volunteered to offer some of his spare time to teach him some basic medical theory. He hardly completed high school. He declined the offer. I was surprised and if I would have been in his shoes, I would have gladly accepted the offer. He secretly told me the reason why did not he accept the offer. He said that "The best doctors would not leave their countries and work on contract in a foreign country. I do not want to learn from a second class doctor". I could read his mind well. It is not the case of everyone. Various other punishing forces are behind their move. Most of the skilled immigrants are pulled, and the refugees are pushed. The Independent classes of immigrants are warmly welcomed, family class immigrants are taken and the refugees are accepted and finally all become equal members of the same family.

In the early days most of the new Immigrants left due to unpleasant situations and could not bear the consequences. It may be a crop failure like in Ireland in the middle of nineteenth century, drought in Ethiopia, war in Sri Lanka, anarchy in Somalia, massacre in Bosnia, human rights violations in some of the Eastern Europe, racial segregation in South Africa. They did not bring pleasant memories. They see their victimization and hardships as a bad dream. Many of the refugees except for economic refugees would not be alive today if they remained in their county of origin, they would have been dead by now.

Brain drain is a common phenomenon between the underdeveloped nations and the developed nations. Some doctors from the province of Ontario moved south of the border for better benefits and salaries, while one million Ontarians do not have the privilege of having family doctors.

Other than necessity, there are positive and negative impacts in having new immigrants from all over the world. The first, is that Canada is able to get services from the new immigrants without making any investment in their growth and education and training. It might not cost as much in Canada compared to some of the developing countries where the standard and the cost of living is comparatively low. But at the Canadian standard, it is pretty high.

There is a long term advantage of these new immigrants. They are mostly middle aged. They are in the stage of having children. Those children will be the potential future human resources. The advantage that we have with the new immigrants is that the sending countries invested on human capital, we get the fruit with no investment cost.

Canada might be in a position today to pick and chose the best ones. Under normal circumstances these ones are one in many. At times we are in a position in getting the best out of the best from some of the supplying countries.

Having a very positive relationship with many nations around the world will certainly help us in developing our foreign policy. This will help us ease tensions, develop better economic relations, promote a higher reputation and get more human resources in the future.

Most of the immigrants at the initial stage do the jobs which the local people do not prefer to do such as demanding, dangerous and dirty jobs that are physically very demanding including seasonal farm jobs. Even some the skilled new immigrants do unskilled or semi skilled jobs. It may take another two generations to find the right job for the right qualifications, skills and experience.

The global village is no longer just a theory; it has become part and parcel of current life. The economic, political, diplomatic and social gates are more widely open than ever before. A typical scène that I had witnessed in the Kennedy subway station is a very good example. In spite of certain differences that these immigrants carried on with them, they had many things in common.

There are some aspects that make the integrating process harder for new immigrants. For example, whenever there is an economic recession or depression, fingers get pointed at new immigrants as a scapegoat. I had seen in the nineties and read that new immigrants were victims of very harsh words and at times were blamed for the economic hardship. It was said that the newcomers and refugees were over dependant on social assistance, they imported crime and they were the primary cause of the increasing violence and so on. This is not the policy of the government and the government does not support these statements. But it hurts the feeling of the new immigrants. It is a type psychological warfare that attempts to discredit them. Some immigrants lost confidence and got into unwanted activities and this produced an adverse reaction nationwide.

The resettlement of newcomers costs Citizenship and Immigration Canada quite a lot. It includes language instruction, resettlement counseling on issues such as integration with the main stream culture of Canada, job retraining, and up to date courses.

The personal advantage for many immigrants is also a contributing factor to their coming to Canada. Better standards of living in Canada are another attraction. The low rates of inflation coupled with low interest rates are also a deciding factor for many immigrants who come from countries where there are no price controls and the cost of buying basic necessities varies from day to day.

In certain cases, new immigrants earn lower wages than their Canadian counterparts but in most cases they earn more compared to their countries of origin. When it comes to employers selecting an employee from Canada versus a new immigrant, his inclination is towards the Canadian. A known person is like your own and old pair of comfortable shoes. In some cases, they prefer the new immigrant in order to communicate with those minority groups. In a similar fashion, the new immigrants when the target their business to the mainstream culture, they prefer to employ mainstream Canadians. There is discrimination in recruitment, wage difference and promotions. Even at the stage of lay off at times they feel they do not deserve it.

Most middle aged males migrate first and then, after they settle down they sponsor the rest of their family. In the early days the main mode of transportation was not by air but by navigation. It was not as safe as today and took a longer period of time sometimes months and in some cases, years. Those men married local women and created new races such as the Métis in Canada, Anglo-Indians in India, Burghers in Sri Lanka, and various mixed races in Latin America.

Migration at the international level was more focused from Europe to the rest of the world in the 19th century. It was a time when Europe was faced with a population explosion and between 1881- 1910 20% of the population increase had been taken by Australia, and North America. Australia, having almost the same size of land as the USA has a population of 20 million today and it was low in the past as well. The migration of Chinese, Indian and other immigrants does not make much of a difference, it accounts for only a small fraction of the fast growing population. But small countries like the Caribbean, migration makes a lot difference in their population. In some of those countries almost half of the natural increase of population emigrated to Canada and other countries.

The emigration in a way reduces the unemployment rate in the sending countries. It is a blessing in disguise. In some cases the frustrated unemployed youth get into illegal activities and increase the crime rate as well. Philippines are one of the world's largest exporters of human resources and Canada has a portion of them. It increases their foreign exchange a bit as well.

Lack of man power is a blessing for the new comers. They have not been considered as a burden or as liabilities rather as assets. At times Canada needs them more than they need Canada. On many occasions it is wise reverse... This question does not arise in many Canadians. When I mention the need for human resources, what I mean is that it depends on the economic strength, natural growth of local population, future economic plans and under utilized resources and the alternative plans for replacing the high ratio of retirees. Considering all these factors Canada annually increases its population by one percent by immigrants from abroad. When the population grows the new immigrant's number also has to be increased. The number of immigrants alone does not matter, the suitable immigrants matter a lot. This does not mean looking for just any highly qualified and skilled worker. There are areas where semi skilled workers are in demand and there is a shortage in the local supply whereas there may be an over supply of workers in certain fields or the need has been met by the local population. For example there was a very high demand for computer science specialists in the 1900s, when the need was very high and local supply was low whereas today, the demand has dropped. After the discovery of new valuable minerals, certainly Canada needs more immigrants. Even in the scale of demand and supply the supply is greater than demand in some categories of man power and the wise reserve some in the other ratio categories. Right now Canada is no longer in need of unskilled labour and seasonal workers. This method of selection has opened the gate wider to the rest of the world. Human capital is the best capital. Today's world has realized that the pen is mightier than any other resource.

The Loyalists were citizens of the American thirteen colonies who wished to remain loyal to the British Empire and emigrated to the provinces of British North America during and post American Revolution of 1775-83. Sixty thousand of them migrated to Canada and five thousand of them Britain and the rest to the West Indies.

The recorded population of Canada during the period of 1851 -1861 was just over three million whereas today's population is over thirty three million. It was the time Canada was not well known to the world it was almost in the hands of two big world powers, the British and French colonies. The Canadian gates were not widely opened to the rest of the world and it was not a unified nation as such. The newcomers did not penetrate deep into the heart of the land. Most of the land remained untouched as forest and grassland. In the absence of an industrialized economy, the rural economy predominantly agriculture and trade moved slowly, and did not require much manpower. The pioneers work hard in clearing the forests, they dug wells, made houses with wood and clay, raised cattle, and built new settlements where had existed. Some of these settlements were in islands like the Thousand Islands in Lake Ontario. Their life was very hard and lonely. Women had to make their own wine, bake their daily bread, sew their own clothes, and maintain the household in general. This life was also fraught with danger for wild animals lived in close proximity to the settlers and were a constant threat. I had a wonderful opportunity to experience such a life when I visited Black Creek Pioneer Village in North Toronto.

At that time people were determined to face and overcome new challenges. They made many initial sacrifices in establishing their new settlements from scratch, with minimal social amenities. In the strange land known as Canada, this was not easy. Many explorers and others who migrated to the new world were attracted by the stories of gold. Once you recognize and try to visualize their struggles, you realize their amazing contribution to today's Canada where we live with many comforts today.

The domination of the cold climate is another discouraging factor that prevented the arrival of newcomers at that time due to the absence of electric heating facilities. Even today with all of the modern facilities and conveniences some immigrants stay in Canada to earn and save substantial mount of money only to return back to the country of their forefathers and settle down. Another group of new skilled immigrants stay for a couple of years to work and gain new experiences and acquire Canadian citizenship and leave for their country of origin.

The bottom line is that there is no way that Canada manages with the natural increase in population. Whether we like it or not new immigrants have to come here. The structure and the system of immigration and the government have convinced us that the constant inflow of new immigrants is unavoidable and should be welcomed.

There was a high rate of new immigrants in the period of 1896 to 1905. One of the main factors that contributed to this was that the government offered free land from the Crown lands. At that time, most of the land was owned or claimed by the government and a portion was in the hands of the First Nations people. Land is the main factor for mining and agriculture. In industry there are four main factors, capital, labour, entrepreneurship and land. Land plays a supranational role, unlike agriculture. Agriculture accounts for just one quarter of the current economy.

When I say land it also includes fresh water such as the Great Lakes, Ocean water, (land 9, 093,507 sq km and the size of water is 891,

163, sq km) space and the minerals married underneath the surface. Fortunately there is no major dispute between the provinces but with the First Nations regarding the ownership of land which has not been fully settled. Though Canada is the second largest country in size (9,984,670 sq km) next to Russia (17, 075, 400 sq km)in the world the suitable land for settlement is only After the discovery of valuable minerals such as crude oil, natural gas, and diamonds in the north the importance of the land in those areas has gone up. Have not territories and provinces have deserted and joined with have provinces. 90% of Canadians live within 320 km of the southern border with USA or in 11% of the total land mass of Canada.

The age of the Canadian land is 3.8 billion years and the first sign of inhabitance was almost 30, 000 years ago. The first Europeans settled in Canada almost 500 years ago; the birth of the Dominion of Canada was 140 years ago, and Newfoundland joined the Canadian Confederation 59 years ago. Canada. Full fledged Canada was born only after Newfoundland joined the confederation. Canada was in existence before this birth of this new nation as a British colony. Canada was not born after a war of independence like a cesarean section. It was an evolutionary birth.

During the First World War the influx of immigrants was very high. After the First World War from 1921-1931 the population grew to over ten million. It was the period after the First World War that mass construction began. It was the return of solders and others who got themselves involved in World War I that contributed to this growth in the population. Constant growth of the population reached twenty million in the period of 1961-1971.

We can see that steady growth in new migration compared with emigration has its own ups and down. When comparing the two (migration with emigration) migration has been higher than emigration. From 1851-1961 and 1891- 1901 the emigration rate was higher than the migration rate. Since 1901-1921 migration has been greater than emigration. In the period of 1931-1941, it was the world wide economic depression that affected Canada along with many other countries. People did not want to take on too many challenges and they might have thought that a` bird in the hand is better than two in the bush". The emigration rate was very low. The migration rate was 1,072,000 and the emigration rate was 149,000. During the period of 1951- 1961 again the emigration number superseded.

So far the peak number of new immigrants arrived in the year of 1913 at 4, 00,870. This was high and reached over three hundred thousand in the years of 1911-1912. In the period of economic depression until the end of the world war 11 (1931-1945) the inflow of new immigrants was very slow. In the 1940's over 48,000 war brides and 22,000 children returned to Canada after the war was over. The returning soldiers and others settled down and started productive economic activities. It was the also the beginning of the baby boom. Since then, the flow of new immigrants has been growing steadily and the baby boomers are becoming seniors today.

In the 1950's the main source of immigrants was Europe though not centered on the United Kingdom and France. The European settlers came from certain concreted areas. They are as follows

a) United Kingdom & France
b) Southern European countries, Italy, Spain, Portugal, Greece
c) Eastern Europe, Poland, Ukraine, Rumania, Hungary, Russia, Serbia, Kosovo, Former Baltic States
d) Scandinavian countries Norway, Sweden, Finland Denmark
e) West European nations, Germany, Switzerland, Luxemburg,

The Immigration act of 1906 and 1910 encouraged the incoming immigrants from certain sections of the globe and swallowed the rest. During the First World War between 1914 -1918 the immigration rate was low

It was in 1928 that the Atlantic gateway wildly opened for the newcomers. It was in 1956-1957 that Hungarian refugees over 37,500 of them were accepted into Canada.

The Immigration gate was opened to many other ethnic groups. The Immigration act of 1962 was very much in favour of many ethnic groups migrating to Canada.

Canada's need for general manpower whether it was skilled labour or unskilled labour, it was accepted. It has been recognized that the need for semi- skilled and skilled manpower are more beneficial than the rest. The point system was introduced in 1967.

In 1968-1969 another influx of refugees of 11,000 came from the former Czechoslovakia. The geographic direction has shifted to Africa, Asia and South America. Another wave of refugees arrived from South America. It was in 1972 under the brutal leader Idi Amin that 6175 Ugandan Asians settled into Canada. Some of them had British passports. They were taken to Uganda and other parts of East Africa and South Africa by their colonial ruler, the British Empire. Chilean refugees over 6000 in number settled in Canada. The Indonesian and the Vietnamese the so called "boat people" arrived in the 1970's. Over 60,000 Vietnamese arrived in 1979-1980. The Sri Lankan and Somalia refugees began to come in the 1980s.

Canada's priorities lean more towards the quality of immigrants rather than the quantity in any category. The evolution of the immigration policy in Canada has taken many paths in reaching today's growth. It has had to dance with international and national challenges such as the abolition of the slave trade, discrimination against certain ethnic groups, the effort to maintain the identity of the mainstream, the between the former Soviet Union and USA, human rights violations, political concepts, cultural concerns, demographic pattern, economic recession and terrorism.

National security, public opinion, international rivalry between the French and British, balancing humanitarian and economic needs; these things that had been considered as the best and right things to consider at one time have turned to be wrong and shameful. Policies and actions that we consider today as barbaric and uncivilized at that time were not considered as such or the gravity of unacceptability was very minute. Therefore we should not measure these things with the current standards.

The main waves of immigrants to Canada can be classified in the following manner:

a) Natives in search of new land for hunting and trading
b) Merchants
c) Craftsmen
d) Asylum seekers and refugees
e) Religious freedom seekers
f) Unskilled workers
g) Semi skilled and skilled workers
h) Family reunion
i) Investors.
j) Economic refugees
k) Illegal Immigrants

One of the important early waves of early European settlers consisted mainly of merchants and craftsmen such as carpenters, blacksmiths, coopers, and joiners. Before the introduction of the industrial revolution, craftsmen occupied the modern skilled worker position. Those early immigrants suffered a lot to build this nation. A strange land sparsely populated. Nothing much to mention of social amenities, poor heating facilities in the winter, no roads, bridges, no public schools, limited medical facilities, and preservation food was a big problem. And in spite of the many challenges that they faced, they worked hard and overcame them and thus brought this nation to a wonderful stage. They deserve more than word of thanks.

The slaves and indentured workers mainly from India and China also added to the Canadian population. The slaves were mainly kept as domestic workers by the high ranking officials and religious communities. Many of them worked in the construction of the railway, clearing lands and on the farms.

A recent survey revealed that one third of the Canadian employers could not find suitable skilled workers to fill the vacancies. The potential skilled workers who migrated into Canada had to face certain barriers in getting into the profession where one had to have acquired a post secondary level of professional education, long years of experiences and more than adequate skills. I do not mean to say that those skilled workers have to be directly engaged in their field of expertise without evaluating their credentials and having updated courses or training completed to suite the needs of the Canadian employers. We all have to acknowledge that the complexity of the Canadian economy and immigration policy requires a better system to meet the fast changing global challenges. This particular Canadian issue is likened to the North American Free Trade Agreement. The United States of America, supplying nations of manpower, provincial governments, human resources development, investors, educators, entrepreneurs, consumers and at large the voters have to play their part. In order to meet the current challenges the immigration policy has to be overhauled, not just by making changes here and there. The current changes are inevitable and this is the first step.

NEW IMMIGRANTS TO CANADA

YEAR	NEW IMM	YEAR	NEW IMM	YEAR	NEW IMM	YEAR	NEW IMM	YEAR	NEW IMM	YEAR	NEW IMM	YEAR	NEW IMM	YEAR	NEW IMM
1860	6276	1880	38,505	1900	41,681	1920	138,824	1940	11,324	1960	104,111	1980	143,117	2000	227,465
1861	13,599	1881	47,991	1901	55,747	1921	91,728	1941	9,329	1961	71,698	1981	128,618	2001	250,638
1862	18,294	1882	112,458	1902	89,102	1922	84,224	1942	7,576	1962	74,586	1982	121,147	2002	229,040
1863	21,000	1883	133,624	1903	138,660	1923	133,729	1943	8,504	1963	93,151	1983	89,157	2003	221,355
1864	24,779	1884	103,824	1904	131,252	1924	124,164	1944	12,801	1964	112,606	1984	88,239	2004	235,824
1865	18,958	1885	79,169	1905	141,465	1925	84,907	1945	22,722	1965	146,758	1985	84,302	2005	262,239
1866	11,427	1886	69,152	1906	211,653	1926	135,982	1946	71,719	1966	194,743	1986	99,219	2006	251,649
1867	10,666	1887	84,526	1907	272,409	1927	135,962	1947	64,127	1967	222,876	1987	152,098		
1868	12,765	1888	88,766	1908	143,326	1928	158,886	1948	125,414	1968	183,974	1988	161,929		
1869	18,830	1889	91,600	1909	173,694	1929	166,783	1949	95,217	1969	164,531	1989	192,001		
1870	24,708	1890	75,067	1910	286,839	1930	104,806	1950	73,912	1970	147,713	1990	241,230		

Year	Value	Year	Value	Year	Value	Year	Value	Year	Value	Year	Value	Year	Value	
1871	27,773	1891	82,165	1911	331,288	1931	27,530	1951	194,391	1971	121,900	1991	230,781	1,678,210
1872	36,578	1892	30,996	1912	375,756	1932	20,591	1952	164,498	1972	122,006	1992	252,842	
1873	50,050	1893	29,633	1913	400,870	1933	14382	1953	168,868	1973	184,200	1993	254,321	
1874	39,373	1894	20,829	1914	150,484	1934	12,476	1954	154,227	1974	218,465	1994	217,950	
1875	27,382	1895	18,790	1915	36,665	1935	11,277	1955	109,946	1975	187,881	1995	212869	
1876	25,633	1896	16,835	1916	55,914	1936	11,643	1956	164,857	1976	149,429	1996	225,313	
1877	27,082	1897	21,716	1917	72,910	1937	15,101	1957	282,164	1977	114,914	1997	216,038	
1878	29,807	1898	31,900	1918	41,845	1938	17,244	1958	124,851	1978	86,313	1998	174,200	
1879	40,492	1899	44,543	1919	107,698	1939	16,994	1959	106,928	1979	112,093	1999	189,966	
TOTAL	485472		1,222,089		3,259,258		11,342		1,973,375		2,813,948		3,475,337	

CHAPTER NINE

INFLUX OF GLOBAL
REFUGEES INTO CANADA

It was my honour to be a guest of the breaking of the Guinness World Record attempt by Suresh Joaeken at the Outlet mall in Mississauga. I happened to be on and off for the three day event. I met with a middle aged refugee lady who was persecuted, tortured and gang raped. She was narrating her story of being victimized with tears flowing like a river from her eyes and exhibited her inner pain and frustration. She was married with a daughter, and was working in a factory as a semi skilled worker. Her husband was one of the active members and involved in trade union activities that has not related to any sort of anti government or politically involved. The army visited on several occasions. She was tortured and her husband was arrested twice. He was tortured so inhumanly that it almost made him paralyzed. She was arrested too and once in broad day light was gang raped. Finally she was able to flee to Canada and gained refugee status. She told me that even after a couple of months after arriving in Canada; she got up in the middle of her sleep and wept. There are numerous pathetic stories beyond these about refugees in Canada.

Other than economic refugees, for all other refugees, it is the last step in order to flee from the country or land where he /she was born and brought up along with their forefathers. These people had been very established in life having deep rooted and sentimental even though the social amenities are limited, the living conditions poor, poor economy, lack of employment. These things do not matter; East or West the home land is the best for them. No man on earth is proud to be branded as a refugee. There is no question of being in between the pulling and pushing forces. There is only one force that makes someone a refugee and that is the pushing force to flee. It is the question of survival from systemic persecution, torture of all kinds, starvation, extra judicial execution, rape, ill treatment, amputation, denial of freedom of expression, jail sentences for innocent civilians. All of these things push these people to come to a strange land where the language, culture, lifestyle, climate, food, religion, ethnicity and the norms of the society are different.

The persecution could be based on religion, race, ethnicity, language, political beliefs, gender, or a combination of these factors and the method and the degree of it may vary but the established danger to life remains the center of focus.   They carry these unforgettable pathetic experiences with them wherever they go. They have witnessed how family members, relatives, and friends suffered, became crippled, massacred, and persecuted. These experiences leave an indelible mark in their hearts and minds and in turn adversely affect the second and third generation. The physiological injuries can be easy assessed but invisible injuries such as Post Traumatic Stress Disorder or depression might not be completely cured and totally erased. Most of these refugees were punished for crimes they did not commit. They suffer at times because of being a member of a designated group. Refugees who were victimized badly, but have no means of fleeing remain and continue to suffer whereas those were victims to a lesser degree were able to flee and gain refugee status. Of course economic refugees who can continue to survive in their home land have not experienced any established persecution, take advantage of the system and undue privileges and occupy the seat meant for true refugees. These economic refugees portray themselves as real victims and abuse the system in order to gain economic benefits. It is very hard in the refugee determination system to decipher this. Although many receiving countries are aware of this problem and improve their systems and minimize the loopholes, no system is able to wipe out this problem.

There are over 25 million refugees and 70 million displaced people, internally and externally around the world. The number has been going upwards and the refugee accepting countries cannot take all of them.

The interesting part of it is that the countries that create refugees also grant asylum to refugees created by the conflicts in another country. An example of this is during the Khalistan war in 1980's. Indian Sikhs fled India as refugees and countries like Canada, Germany, Britain, and France accepted them as refugees. Interestingly enough, refugees from Afghanistan and Pakistan got asylum in India.

The refugee policies of most of the accepting countries are almost the same and are based on the 1951 UN Convention on the protection of refugees. This UN Convention defines a refugee as someone who has a well founded fear of persecution because of race, religion, nationality, membership in a social group, or political opinion. In the 1990's in Canada some groups of people advocated to include persecution based on gender and so far, no input has been made. It is hoped that this idea has not blown away with the wind. Our system is very flexible and covers all types of persecution in general. It is the suffering from the individualized persecution, not generalized persecution that is taken into account. The violence or persecution must be directed to the refugee claimant not in general. Refugees fleeing from generalized violence would not be accepted as refugees. The victim of a bomb blast targeted not to him in particular, but to a rebel controlled area may not be sufficient cause for him to be qualified to be a refugee and the claim may be refused. In a bomb blast it could happen to anyone. Canada is the only major refugee receiving country that accept refugees on permanent exile, the rest accept them temporarily until the situation is determined to be safe. Bottom-line of the Canadian refugee exercise is aimed at resettlement whereas most of the other receiving nations give protection until they will be able to return back to their respective countries sooner or later. Depending on the circumstances, in Canada a refugee claimant is accepted as conventional refugee, the next step will be permanent resident status and in two or three year's time moving to apply for naturalized citizenship. Those who do not meet the refugee criteria but are not a burden to Canada, are economically independent, and have a valid reason for being unable to return to their homeland would be able to absorbed as permanent residents under humanitarian and compassionate grounds.

Though the definition that almost all countries use as a yard stick to determine refugees, the interpretation varies according to the government. A rejected refugee claim of a person with the same or similar evidence might gain refugee status in another country. That is one of the reasons that many refugees enter through the land border between the USA and Canada to claim refugee status, but many prefer to come to Canada for various reasons such as free health services, having relatives residing in Canada and so on. The fundamental reason is that they believe that the accepting ratio is higher in Canada than in the States and is a safe heaven for refugees. A refugee who wants to escape from a dangerous situation and save his life would not pick and choose. Suppose someone flees from Somalia to Canada by flight and it was on transit in Paris, France, he should break his journey and claim refugee status in France, not in Canada.

Internal flight alternatives are another concept that limits the influx of refugees. Someone's life is in danger in a particular part of a nation but he could survive in another part of the same nation, therefore he would not be considered as a refugee.

Asylum counties are reluctant to condemn source countries that are also a friend or ally but a refugee is more likely to receive protection in an enemy country. Most of the asylum countries are Western Europe, USA, Canada and Australia. They are biased against communist countries. Refugee claimants who flee from Communist countries have a better chance than from the anti communist block. For example after the Second World War until the collapse of the Communist regime in Eastern Europe, Vietnam, China, North Korea and Cuba refugees were easily accepted. It was more or less to stop the expansion of communist ideology to third world countries. There is no doubt that most of the fundamental freedoms such as freedom of expression, press, has died in those countries and in some cases people who should be included were excluded and excluded were included. In many cases of the refugees who were fleeing from communist countries, they were accepted mainly not because of personalized persecution but generalized persecution whereas refugees from non communist countries had to go through the bottle neck of the system. The ratio of the asylum seekers from those countries is higher than the rest. I do not think the application of the refugee system is fair to the deserving cases. The political ideology should not interfere or dominate on the refugee determination system. When a government officer flees his country he is treated as defectors, whereas the sportsmen from Cuba who recently disappeared and eventually claimed refugee status, they and other common men who are in the same boat are treated differently. It should be that no matter who he is, everybody is equal in front of the law and I do not think there should be an exception or preferential treatment

Some economic refugees and others who do not meet the entry criteria abuse the system and joint the crowed of refugees as a short cut and eventually gain the permanent resident visa. USA has an alternative system for those who want to be green card holders by joining the immigration lottery system that has lesser qualifications to get in than the others. But Canada does not have such a lottery.

Every receiving country has a quota for refugees, among those countries Canada comparatively accepts more refugees than others. Is it an obligation for a nation to accept a certain number of refugees or should it be optional to the sovereign state? It is hard to define how it should work. The world's refugees total number, and destination would not be not able to predict though it is an issue that is being created by fellow human beings

There are some practical difficulties that receiving nations have to face and resolve in the best interest of the nation. A good example is that when Bill Clinton, the former President of the USA wanted to get rid of most of the illegal immigrants Canada went on alert because many of those illegal immigrants would go on a mass exodus to Canada under the pretext as refugees. Fortunately the proposal was given up, maybe so as not to lose Spanish American vote. When one receiving country makes it difficult, other receiving countries are loaded with an influx of refugees.

There is a big back log in processing refugee applications. For example, in Canada in the year 1981 the back lock was 81, 000. It was not only caused by the lack of insufficient facilities and manpower but the influx of a high number of refugee claimants and the delaying tactics of the refugee's and in some cases the handlers as well. They did at one point in time make the processing faster and easier, so that many positive results could be delivered or general animosity given as it was given in May 1986. The Jews on the board the ship fleeing Nazi Germany were refused by country after country, each refusal made a stronger case for refusal by other countries.

So called "boat people" were refugees who sailed in small boats into Canada from Vietnam and most of them were accepted as refugees, whereas the 174 Sikhs from India who arrived in a Chilean registered freighter The Amelie on the shore Nova Scotia from West Germany, Belgium, and Netherlands were tuned back.

After the September 11, 2001 terrorist attacks in the United States the case of the acceptance of refugees has been restricted and it is harder than ever before. The refugees cannot be expected to comply with the immigration regulations at the time of having to safeguard their life from an established persecution every minute. They would not be able to secure the proper legal documents before fleeing. If he can get those documents from his government, at times he can be considered a refugee. Forging the travel documents and fleeing was accepted to an extent but these days most of the western countries do not entertain forged travel document of the receiving country. It is because of past experience, some terrorists disguised as refugees entered Canada and somehow snuck into the USA and got involved in destructive activities against the U.S and aimed at some other nations that support them and where their network are in operation. There are people who engaged in illegal businesses such as smuggling drugs, weapons, and people.

Refugees arrive in three categories. The refugees who enter into the boarder by land, ocean and by air illegally in the sense of having no entry visa. They account for almost one third of the total refugee population of Canada. After the Canadian government signed the safe third country agreement the number of undocumented immigrants has been reduced drastically. The second group selects refugees abroad and shoulders the responsibilities of their resettlement by private non profit and charitable organizations.

The third category of refugees is government sponsored. The government is directly involved in selecting these refugees abroad and helps them resettle in Canada. They are able to gain permanent resident status immediately or sooner than the refugee claimant who arrived or reached the border and knocked at the gate. Since all of them are already selected as refugees there is no room for reselection and some are turned back.

The increasing number of refugees around the world cannot be totally resolved. But it can be helped by accepting nations allocating more resources, determining a better way of identifying real refugees and hiring well trained skilled workers to conduct this procedure along with timely processing. Not overburdening to a few countries like Canada and taking a fair share would also ease the burden. It is only a cure but the preventive methods would reduce the number of innocent citizens becoming refugees.

CHAPTER TEN

FROM CONFRONTATION
TO COMPROMISE

I was on my vacation in a beautiful sub tropical island in the Caribbean after the 40th federal election, in which had I participated by endorsing a couple of candidates belonging to our party. It so happened that my partner in playing a chess game was a French citizen who took a great interest in Canadian issues, especially Quebec. Sometimes we conversed late into the night and these conversations prompted me to write this article regarding the issue of Québec sovereignty and federalism in Canada.

I have a very special attachment and fascination with both the St Lawrence River and the cosmopolitan city of Montreal because of some very sweet memories. When I came to Canada and landed in Montreal, I was welcomed very cordially. The second reason is that when I was attending high school in my country of origin in the tropics, my geography teacher pointed out the St. Lawrence River and the city of Montréal on a map. My teacher explained that at that time Montreal was the biggest city in Canada, and told us that during the winter, the river would freeze solid and people could walk on it. Now, being a person who had never even seen a snowflake, I could not believe this story and it became my dream to one day walk on the same frozen river and it came true.

I am pretty aware that Quebec sovereignty is a very old, sensitive, and pressing issue that has to be resolved sooner rather than later with a solution that benefits all Canadians from coast to coast. Nicolas Sarkozy the president of France, and the current chairman of the European Union while in attendance of the summit of the Francophonie in Québec City, paid an official visit to the residence of the Governor General and stated that the relationship between France and Quebec is like that of brothers while the relationship with Canada is between friends. The former French president Charles de Gaulle had also made a similar comment "Long live the friendship between Canada and France. Long live the brotherhood between the French people and Quebec people". He further said in Montreal during a state visit to Canada for Expo 67 and the Canadian centennial celebrations "Vive le Quebec libre ". I would prefer to view our relationship between Canadians of various ethnicities and Quebecers as cousins and the rest of us as newly wedded brides of the mainstream. Anglophone culture. That way, no one is kept out of this extended family relationship we call Canada.

If Canada had become the 14th colony of America, this crisis of defining the relationship between the French and the British would not have arisen. We would have been considered members of a new family called America and English would have been the only official language. Thank God it never happened. I can imagine what would have happened if thirteen colonies adopted the Canadian policy of multiculturalism, there would have been numerous crises. America once made an offer to Quebec to become part of their nation as a14th colony, invaded the territory and practically captured Quebec City. But, the Quebecers decided to remain with the British. In the beginning of the 17th century, amongst the French immigrants, one third was military personnel who wanted to settle abroad whereas the American British population was 1.5 million.

The constitutional change of 1791 split the colony into Upper Canada and Lower Canada and gave equal representation in the assembly, irrespective of the size of the demographic pattern .Even after the formation of a single government in 1840, it continued.

Equal representation is not an exclusive issue between Quebecers and the federal government, as sovereignty versus federation, unity versus separation, minority versus majority or a historical accident. Nor is it an issue of a minority in the Quebecois population who are advocating for due or undue rights. Rather it is a constitutional matter that concerns all Canadians. This issue can certainly and should be resolved by Canadians and for the Canadian extended family inclusive of Quebecers. Please note, in the rest of this article Canadians refers to both the Quebecers and the rest of Canadians. The barometer of the results of the past referendums in Quebec presented by the provincial governments indicated that the majority of the Quebecers wanted to remain in Canada. We should not take it for granted that the ones who voted against the referendum have totally accepted the current federal system of government as it is without any decentralization and rebalance of power. There is no guarantee that the reading of the tea leaves will remain positive and the result of the last referendum was won by the federal government by less than a percentage. I have observed that the integration and disintegration of nations has two main causes, coupled with many others. They are ethnic identity and economic factors; the ratio between the two varies, in many circumstances.

The French are in general more focused and centralized in their ethnic identity and maintain roots in France. This was witnessed during historical times including the colonial era, when the British and French empires competed with each other in conquering various parts of the world The colonial administration of the British operated through the reorganization of local leaders and administrated their power through them as a form of indirect rule. The French however, centralized their administrative powers and the nature of the colonial administration was focused on responsibility to France. It was said that when it was raining in France, people in the French colonies spread out the umbrella. Though this is an exaggeration, there is an element of truth in it. Quebec was heavenly dependant on France. France had overall control of the new French colony both economically and politically. In 1746, the fur trade was the main source of employment and 47% of the trade was controlled by French companies and its agencies. The local people enjoyed little benefit and remained poor, but the money generated by the trade was spent lavishly.

For the early French settlers, the Roman Catholic faith had a very high influence, more in the realm of political decision making and governance than spiritual life. The Church was directly involved in governing the colony and the Bishop was one of three members of the ruling council and he had a very high influence in making decisions and executing them. The French settlers did not have any religious discrimination or persecution of their immigrants compared to some of the British settlers.

Historically, the Quebecers and the British settlers in the new world established their settlements and made their way of living by themselves. But the colonial masters of the British and the French fought and transferred the power between themselves and the original partition was made. The French settlers were the ones who named this nation "Canada". They were the first European settlers in this portion of North America. The Québec Act of 1774 recognized the French language, the Roman Catholic faith and the civil rights of the inhabitants. When confederation was proclaimed, Quebec was considered an equal partner, not one among the four provinces.

Quebec has been encouraged to protect, maintain, promote and practice the French cultural values, language, identity, arts and traditions, though the concept of multi-culturalism was officially proclaimed and practiced and bi-lingualism has been in practice all over Canada. The Quebecers are given a special status, as a distinguished society, a nation within a united Canada, although Bloc Quebecois Leader Gilles Duceppe, during the 2008 federal election campaign debate claimed that the recognition of Quebec as nation does not have any constitutional blessing. The English language version of Right Hon. Prime Minister's refers to them as 'Quebecois' but some expect to be referred to as 'Quebecers' Former Prime Minister Lester Pearson stated that 'while Quebec is more than a province because it is the heartland of a people, in a very real sense it is a nation within a nation.' Canadians are carefully reviewing the terms of this issue and it has been referred to as 'sovereignty', 'autonomy', 'self determination', 'ethnocentric "constitutional reforms', and 'Quebec's independence struggle'.

This struggle continued in a cold ballet against fiery bullets in October 1970 during the Quiet Revolution. The blowing external wind of independence movements in Africa and some parts of Europe passed through middle class radicals. The growth of the middle class made a significant impact on the socio-economic structure of Quebec. The migration of these people from rural farms to urban areas substantiated influential force. They were the first terrorists in Canadian history, but it subsided and died a natural death.

The definitions of 'nation and 'state' in political terms has a wide range of meaning. A nation could be based on region, ethnicity, language, race, religion and still be part of a sovereign state whereas a state is an independent entity. In the United States of America, 'states' refers to not a part equal to the federal government, rather under the jurisdiction of the federal government. Nation in the Canadian context does not refer to 2 different independent states. Rather it refers to the Federal system of governance. The Canadian constitution is neither a fully written constitution like that of the USA nor the British constitution which is mainly unwritten. Our constitution borrows elements of both. Although there were some changes in 1940, 1951 and 1964 and amendments made in the constitution of 1867 until the *Constitution Act* of May 17 1982 there were no structural changes made. The most important part of the evolution of the Canadian constitution was that Quebec did not sign on to the *Constitution Act* of 1982.

Let me pinpoint some of the visible and hidden concerns of some if not many, Quebecers as follows.

1) Quebecers are not treated equally but as second class citizens
2) Quebecers are not treated as second class citizens but less privileged
3) Quebec identity is precious and it can not be blended or mixed with another
4) Quebec's sovereignty can not be compromised; it is alive and matter of time.
5) What is the guarantee for the special status of Quebec in the future?
6) Quebecers would be better if it is a sovereign state

7) Does Canada get more from Quebec than the wise reverse
8) Identity cannot be compromised with economic advantages.
9) Being together is a historical accident and has to be rectified
10) Disintegration is a process of 1990s and will have to continue
11) It is not a process of separation, but to regain what has been lost.

The first two opinions are very comparable to the non-French speaking. Specifically English speaking Canadians in Quebec, with the one million Quebecers in the rest of Canada do not differ much in terms of rights and privileges. If they are not more than parallel, they are not lower than in the rest of Canada. Historically speaking at the time when new settlements were established by the French and British, the size of the population, growth and political power would have been parallel but when Quebec joined with the rest of the three provinces in forming the confederation, although the same status was given, democratically and in terms of economic strength, Quebec lost most of its original status.

The world has changed drastically and the victory of Barack Obama in the American presidential race in November 2008 is a very solid example of superseding economic interest over racial, ethnically biased actions. Apartheid was destroyed by a crucial war in the land of the blacks accounting for over 80% of its population, whereas in the States, equal status at the top position was whole heartily granted by the white majority. These days money speaks louder than the rest.

France and the rest of the European Union at the initial stage, mainly focused on economic cooperation amongst themselves and later on they realized that all aspects of life are interrelated, interdependent and insupportable with the economy and thus extended their focus into other areas such as; establishing a common European currency, developing an interrelated immigration policy and creating a similar or common foreign policy. Though it is too early to comment because the European Union has been in existence for no more that two decades; history has proven that some or one of the member nations can reach the level of super power, or move into a different political camp such as communism or socialism and the mode of production can shift to state control and a one party system or dictatorship emerges. The influence of globalization has diluted the hard core of cultural demarcation and ethnic identity. The quest for identity is subsiding. The so-called modern civilization which is not necessarily the exclusive version of George W. Bush, has been penetrating all over the world and warmly accepted in many places and tolerated by some conservatives. When it comes to establishing the modern civilization, the French are both contributing to it and sharing from the rest of it.

I appreciate the past generation of Quebecers whose life was mostly influenced by the Roman Catholic faith; one example is that most of them practice family planning and attended church regularly, whereas now there is a remarkable change brought by modern civilization. Declining in the practice of the Roman Catholic faith contributed to the radical decline in the birth rate. Quebec had the highest birth rate in Canada and soon had the lowest

The second main factor that is pushing sometimes and pulling back at others is the economic interdependency, strength, weakness and revelation. Economic factors have a higher degree of influence around the world proportionally speaking. The integration, union of nations and disintegration of unions are also based on economic reasons. The disintegration of Soviet Union was caused by various factors, the economic disaster being one of the major ones. Historically, Quebec was not self sufficient and this was a big drawback. Quebec's strength in being united with Canada is high no matter what the sate of the national or international economy. One of the main concerns of a common man in Quebec is centralized towards economic advantages, such as employment, higher wages to meet the effects of inflation, tax relief and so on. Almost 40% of the Quebecers are low or middle income earners and most of them do not pay significant income taxes.

The worst case scenario, which I would not want to experience, is that if Quebec were to separate, it would be a disaster for both the Quebecers and the rest of Canada. Quebec separation would weaken the economy and politically two nations would have to suffer the consequences. Canada is located beside a strong English speaking nation, the United States. Quebec would be sandwiched by the two nations and America may engage in a game of triangle politics by fueling the enmity between the two to gain advantages from them both and I do not wish elaborate more on it.

The second major problem is that the First Nations will reclaim their land rights and Quebec will have to face another fight and will go back to the small parcel of land that it was it had at the time of Confederation. The current size of Quebec is much larger than the time when it joined confederation.

If any of this happens it is going to be the beginning of an end, not the end of an end. Some of the "have" provinces would follow suite not on the primary basis of ethnicity but on the strength and interest of economic and regional inclinations.

The Canadian constitution in regards to unilateral separation has more flexibility and it has to be taken into consideration. The *Clarity Act* of 1999 set out the conditions under which the federal government would enter into discussions following a vote by any province. The Act gave the Canadian Parliament the power to decide whether a proposed referendum question was considered clear, and allowed the elected representatives of all Canadians from all provinces and territories to decide whether a clear majority had expressed itself in any referendum. It is widely considered by sovereigntists as indefensible, and in this case, inapplicable. In fact, it is sanctioned by the UNO. A contradictory, but non-binding and symbolic Act representing the exercise of the fundamental rights and prerogatives of the Quebec people and the province of Quebec was introduced in the national assembly of Quebec two days after the *Clarity Act* had been introduced in the House of Commons.

I do not consider this is an exclusive issue of Quebecers, rather it is a national issue in which the concerns and contributions by every Canadian is highly appreciated. The advocates of Quebec sovereignty, Quebec, and the rest including other Quebecers are not in a rivalry camp. There is no doubt that Quebecers have some justification and excuses for demanding more from the national cake and more rights in preserving their identity and the matter of constitution can be addressed in a constitutional manner with open heart and not only look into the past and present situation within the national boundaries, but also the effects that we are bound to get from international changes and forces. There is no enmity in the question of sovereignty, it is a matter that has to be discussed and resolved as members of the same family.

The world is changing rapidly; countries that bitterly fought against each other have joined together and progressed. Germany, France, The United Kingdom and Italy, horribly fought in different camps and most of them are members of the European Union, and members of NATO. Britain under Blair's government was the right hand man during the Iraq war and Canadian Prime Minster Chrétien was almost a stranger to American President George W. Bush. When Bush thanked the world's leaders who helped him during the aftermath of the 9-11 terrorist attacks, he did not even bother to mention Canada and later on brought lame excuses. During the American Revolution they considered the British Empire as their enemy and now we are good friends.

What is going to be the remedy, it is not that simple as the question being asked. It is going to be neither the side of sovereignty nor the current federalist approach. There must be certain fundamental change in the federal constitution based on the input from all Canadians. It has been said in many corners of Canada that more powers have been centralized and given in the hands of he federal government and the provincial governments wants to have decentralized power and rebalance to the provinces. The equilibrium is very hard to make and there are pros and corns either way. The stronger the federal government, the better for bargaining and establishing ourselves globally and the nation as a whole will benefit from a decentralized system of government which will allow for more individual freedom.

CHAPTER ELEVEN

CANADA'S ACCOMMODATIVE IMMIGRATION POLICY, PRINCIPLES AND PHILOSOPHY

"Immigration policy is the outcome of an interactive process at the national level that incorporates information based on the country's actual experience with immigrants, as well the perception of policy-making elites regarding the role of immigration and desirability." These words by Kritz and Nogle, immigration-policy critics, inspired me to write this article. The evolution of Canada's immigration policy, philosophy and principles is interesting and unique, and is incomparable with that of any of the countries whose people we accept as new Canadians.

The complexity of designing and implementing successful immigration policy is much more sensitive than that of virtually every other policy-making department in that it includes elements of both the public and private sectors. Human resources, settlement, education, health, economics, law enforcement, employment, the shortage or over-abundance of local workers, demand and supply, real estate, international trade and workers' mobility—many elements of life in this country are affected by immigration.

On account of its social and economic importance, every step made at the right time in the right direction can bring great benefit to our society. I am of the opinion that, although current immigration policy has been revised and amended, a fundamental overhaul of the Immigration Act of 1976 is overdue. In the three decades since it was adopted, a lot of change has taken place, often quite rapidly, especially in technology, demographic patterns, international trade and the type of immigration that Canada requires. These days, investors, immigrants of the independent class and skilled workers make up almost half the annual total of newcomers. This is based on the needs of the economy more than on any other factor. Particularly in the West, in today's global market skilled workers are in high demand in some sectors while in other sectors the demand is lower. On the other hand, educated, experienced and skilled workers have to overcome many hurdles before their credentials are accepted. The federal government is working hard to change this.

Canada is becoming more and more diverse in terms of its population. Ethnicity, demographics, religion, language and heritage values are more varied than ever before, and almost 20% of today's Canadians were born outside the country to non-Canadian parents.

Immigration policy must be adapted to the times. Certain policies might have worked successfully at one time but are outdated now. For example, during the Brian Mulroney era, there was a suggestion that new immigrants be assigned to specific non-urban areas at the initial stage of their arrival and permitted to move later on to the cities of their choice, should they wish to do so. Upon closer study, the plan was seen to be fraught with problems and the idea was dropped. When Paul Martin was the prime minister, it was proposed that a plan allowing a family member in any category to be sponsored be instituted—providing that the individual being proposed met the criteria for acceptance to this country. However, in this instance, too, the proposal was deemed unfeasible and was subsequently abandoned.

Throughout the history of Canada, the nation has been under-populated. This under-population was keenly felt, particularly during World Wars One and Two, and during the hard-hitting economic depression of 1939. New immigrants were particularly welcomed during these periods. Nowadays, due to the low rate of natural population growth, Canada needs new immigrants to help build up a stronger economic base. Normally people tend to migrate for mainly economic reasons. They want to leave countries of lower productivity for those that have higher productivity as these richer countries offer them far greater economic opportunity as well as enriched educational possibilities for their children.

In the past, immigration policy was geographically and racially biased. Those most welcome included whites from Great Britain, the United States and parts of Western Europe, especially France. Then the circle widened to include the citizens of other Western European nations—with certain conditions attached. These criteria included good health, good character and skills that would benefit the Canadian economy. Potential immigrants' being able to easily integrate into Canadian society was also a valued quality. The demand that these criteria be met set up innumerable barriers and restrictions to would-be immigrants who were white or non-white, and skilled or unskilled.

The beautiful baby, Canada, was born healthy with full strength, but its deficiency in terms of human resources held it back then and, to a lesser degree, still tends to hold it back. Sir John A. Macdonald took the initiative to change things, but no instant response was forthcoming because of the economic depression of 1873-96. Immigration rates eventually rose, but began to improve only in the 1890s. The initiatives taken to expand the Canadian agricultural sector in particular and overall economy in general coincided with a population explosion in Europe. Therefore, at this time the Government of Canada encouraged new settlement in the Midwest. Crown lands were distributed that granted a quarter section of free land of 160 acres to any settler 21 years of age or older who paid a ten-dollar registration fee, resided on his quarter section for three years, cultivated 30 acres and built a permanent dwelling.

Along with the allocation of Crown lands, another positive element that opened up the Midwest was the construction of the Canadian Pacific Railway (CPR) in the 1880s. Although the Crown lands were but a small portion of the total land mass of this country, the farming that was undertaken there had a strong impact on Canada's economy. The government advertised the sale of land in Europe and in the United States, seeking newcomers to build up the country. Sir John A. Macdonald regarded America as a rival nation when it came to attracting new immigrants. However, between 1901 and 1914, more than 750,000 migrants crossed the U. S. border and settled in Canada. Fully one-third of these originally came from Germany, Hungary, Norway, Sweden and Iceland. By the time they arrived in Canada, they were familiar with North American life. Many brought with them the farming experience they had gained on the American prairies. Therefore, they were able to integrate well, and quickly became successful in the Canadian Midwest.

Even at that stage, not every applicant from America who technically met the criteria was accepted. For example, all applications submitted by blacks were rejected, although such discrimination was allegedly based on Canada's having already accepted thousands of freed black slaves who had been admitted to this country as loyalists of the British Empire. And, even earlier than that, countless runaway slaves had obtained refuge in Canada.

It is indisputable that the white settlers of the prairies wanted that land for whites only. Ostensibly, at the core of this was the idea, more or less, of maintaining and preserving homogeneous heritage values, and not having people of other ethnicities around to dilute those values—particularly black people. The Edmondson municipal council, for example, passed a resolution urging the federal government to "take all action necessary to prevent the expected influx of Negroes." In today's dictionaries even the word Negro is pejorative.

The Immigration Act of 1952 did not make any truly significant changes to the previous Immigration Act of 1910 in that the Cabinet still held the reins in terms of decision-making as to who would be accepted into the country. Claims were made that Canada's climate was "unsuitable" for people of certain ethnic backgrounds, and that many of these people did not have the ability to adapt to Canadian ways. However, when Soviet forces brutally crushed the Hungarian Revolution in 1956, Canada accepted 38,000 out of over 200,000 people who applied. Many Canadians, particularly Quebeckers, warmly welcomed the newcomers, most of whom were Catholics like them. And, of course, these people were white.

Still, those who were against accepting such large numbers of Hungarians were unhappy about bringing in many of these refugees—and they were refugees by international definition—because their country of origin was socialist and because it was a member of the Warsaw Pact.

In 1957 the number of immigrants arriving in Canada was 282,164, and, in the subsequent few years, just over 100,000 people came here. At this time the quality of the immigrants accepted rose along with the quantity. Initially, only the ability to perform manual labour was required, while, later on, farming skills and craftsmen's skills were seen as highly desirable. Then, in the 1940s and 1950s, Canada began to seek out semi-skilled and skilled immigrants. Subsequently, the search was on for professionals, and so it remains today: Canada continues to welcome more and more semi-skilled and skilled workers as well as doctors, dentists, engineers, teachers, financial professionals and IT specialists.

These days, the decentralization of power and the allocation of certain powers of immigration have become very important issues. As U.S Barack Obama declared at the convention when he accepted his party's nomination during his campaign, Americans need to put America first—before party politics. The same holds true of us in Canada. We must put Canada first and then, and only then; consider our own region of the country or our respective cultural backgrounds.

Speaking of Mr. Obama, it is interesting to note that, in a recent interview, the Democratic candidate for the US presidency said that his "racial identity is not the core of who I am." Indeed, Obama considers himself part of a "post-racial" world—a world where, truly, race does not matter while the way a person conducts himself, in terms of his value system and his actions, is the important thing. This is an important lesson that the whole world needs to learn, and, thankfully, the world is slowly grasping that this is the only way to reduce strife and work together for the common good.

Tragically, however, discrimination based on race was the rule until fairly recently and, of course, its insidious influence continues to be felt all over the world. Let's look at Canada. Until 1978, our immigration policy gave significantly preferential treatment to some ethnic groups while denying access to others. The Canadian Immigration Act of 1910 and the law passed in 1919 permitted Cabinet to bar certain groups by branding them as "undesirables, owing to their peculiar customs, habits, modes of life and methods of holding property, and because of their probable inability to become readily assimilated." This authority was sealed in an Order in Council on March 14, 1919, and it denied entry to Canada to Germans, Austrians, Hungarians and Bulgarians except for those who were granted special permission by the minister of immigration.

If certain groups of white Europeans were unwelcome on these shores at that time, one can imagine how people of colour were viewed. Nevertheless, change, which is inevitable, did come about and is ongoing. The first visible minorities who were let into the country were, as is well known, actively discriminated against, but still, more and more kept arriving over the years as Canadian society evolved and matured. Now, of course, Canada—especially urban Canada—is a kaleidoscope of many different colours of people from all over the world.

Despite this discrimination, however, which existed in virtually every "white" country in the world in the past, Canada was the first receiving nation to remove it from its immigration system. Since February 1, 1967, all qualified people have been welcomed into this country. A point system was introduced whereby potential immigrants (not refugees) were evaluated as to their suitability to enter and to participate in building up this great nation. Whoever achieves the requisite marks in terms of the point system, irrespective of ethnicity or cultural background, is granted immigrant status.

Canadian immigration policy can be divided into three distinct stages: from confederation to the 1960s, from that time until the 1980s, and subsequently up to today. Citizenship is another important aspect of the immigration system. Holding Canadian citizenship is the birthright of everyone born here and an honour to those who have become naturalized citizens. In some countries, if a baby is born to non-citizens, the child does not have the right of citizenship by birthright.

Babies born in those countries are considered to hold the citizenship of their parents. In Canada, however, the situation is different. Even if a child is born on Canadian soil to rejected refugee applicants, that child is a full-fledged Canadian citizen. Should the child's parents be deported, he still has the rights and privileges of every other Canadian. Upon his reaching adulthood, if the child wants to sponsor his parents, he has to meet the family-class sponsorship criteria to bring them back into the country. As well, the child can come and go as he wishes on his Canadian passport.

Since February 15, 1977, the Citizenship Act has deemed that all naturalized citizens have rights equal to those who were born in Canada. It's different in the United States. Although naturalized Americans enjoy many citizenship rights, some rights are denied them. When President Richard Nixon was removed from his post after the Watergate scandal, Henry Kissinger, the Secretary of State, was at the height of his influence and power. However, because he was born abroad and was a naturalized citizen, he could not run for presidential office as the US Constitution states that only an individual born in the USA can hold the nation's highest office.

There are, of course, several exclusions of certain would-be immigrants to Canada. No-one who is peripherally or directly involved in criminal activity is accepted. Having a medical condition that would place undue stress on Canada's health-care system also disqualifies a candidate. (Numerous court cases have challenged this policy, with varying results.)

Political and economic realities are the primary criteria when it comes to accepting newcomers. Economics heavily influences politics and vice-versa. For example, Canada does not refuse people from countries whose politics differ vastly from ours. Our troops are fighting the Taliban in Afghanistan, and we readily accept those Afghans who are fleeing the insurgents—after doing due diligence as to where their political loyalties lie. Canada did not support Soviet policies when the USSR was one of the strongest alliances on earth, but accepted many Ukrainian farmers. During the most recent recession, in the 1990s, when it became necessary to forge closer economic ties with China, the prime minister put China's human rights' violations aside and dealt with the economic issues with which he had to deal. Times are different now, and it was felt by many that Canada did right to speak out about these violations at the time of the Beijing Olympics.

As we have stated before, Canada needs vast numbers of newcomers to build up its economic base. For example, the USA has a population of 350 million in a smaller land mass than Canada. We have a population of approximately 33 million. The Americans accept more people annually than Canada does, and, as everybody knows, the American economy is far richer than ours. The facts speak for themselves.

In my view, the philosophy behind Canada's immigration policy is the one of the most important components of our national philosophy. It is summarized briefly below:

1) Canada does not compromise on its core values, established by the founding fathers of this great nation.

2) Canada respects human values and accommodates refugees on purely humanitarian grounds, even when it is difficult for us to accept some of these people.

3) Canada always plans ahead and tries to foresee the future before taking action.

4) Canada has superb tolerance and positive attitudes towards people of other backgrounds.

5) Canada accepts new immigrants and refugees with dignity and respect for who they are. It never directly nor indirectly influences them to detach themselves from their heritage values.

In all of these aspects, Canada is a role model for the entire world. It is for these reasons, and many more, that so many people from every corner of the globe wish to come here and start new lives. We have earned our reputation; let's do our best to maintain it.

CHAPTER TWELVE

MY SCARBOROUGH

It was a very pleasant dinner party in downtown Toronto. I was invited as a guest, and was seated next to a highly skilled, recently-arrived new immigrant from East Asia whom I knew quite well. While having dinner, we started chatting about various topics, and, in due course, our conversation turned to real estate. The gentleman next to me told me he was looking to buy a house. I said, "Why don't you look for one in Scarborough?"

Spontaneously his face turned bright red, and a sharp, bitter reaction poured out of him. He spoke very negatively about Scarborough, and his vehemence shocked me. I would never have expected a new immigrant to react in such a manner. I knew it was unlike him to express himself like that and realized that someone must have given him a biased opinion.

I buried my emotional reaction within myself and told him quietly that I had been living in Scarborough for the past 21 years and have never had any trouble. Rather, I told him, I enjoy living here. He told me that his friends had advised him that Scarborough should be his last choice. This is how a wonderful place is being painted with the wrong color.

Scarborough is a world in miniature. One can easily see this at Kennedy Station during rush hour. People who live and work in Scarborough come from over 170 countries, speak more than 160 languages and come from a multitude of ethnic groups. They live together like members of a modern family. Indeed, Scarborough is a role model for multiculturalism—the concept of unity in diversity, of people living together in peace and harmony. The demographic composition of Scarborough is special and unique. One need not travel around the world in eighty days to have new experiences. One need only visit Scarborough for a few hours to be exposed to a world of international culture and cosmopolitan experiences.

Today's rainbow in Scarborough reflects its make-up very well. It came out from a single cloud. When a couple of pioneers, David and Mary Thomson, settled in Scarborough almost 170 years ago, it was virgin forest land. Since then, much transformation has taken place. Scarborough became part of Metropolitan Toronto on January 1, 1998, when the cities of Etobicoke, North York, York, East York and Toronto were amalgamated, and when the outlying boroughs, including Scarborough, were brought into the amalgamation. Now Scarborough is part of the Greater Toronto Area (GTA), an area of **6387 sq km** with a population of 2,385,421. The size of Scarborough is 70 sq miles.

Beneath our topsoil lie layers of Pleistocene deposits of the Great Ice Age, thousands of feet thick. Under them are the Ordovician sedimentary rocks. This rock formation contains fossils that were brought by the invasion of the sea more than 500 million years ago. It is land rich in minerals and fertile soil. The Scarborough landscape reflects the richness of what lies beneath the surface of the ground. Its magnificent cliffs and lakes, coupled with the great variety of trees such as maple, walnut, birch, oak and magnolia add to the beauty. In spring and summer, grass in all its glory covers the ground like a rich carpet. In winter, the purity of the snow covers all and imparts the landscape with a bare and haunting beauty. Beautiful Lake Ontario and the other Great Lakes did not exist before the Pleistocene Ice Age. The Ice Age created not only the large lakes, but the numerous small lakes, rivers and creeks that are such an important part of where we live. They are part of Scarborough as well.

The first inhabitants of Scarborough were the natives who migrated to North America from Siberia via the Alaskan land bridge, which no longer exists. Research indicates that they arrived on our shores between 30,000 and 35,000 years ago. Their main occupations were hunting and trading. They began to make things around 5000 BCE. Around 500 BCE, agriculture was introduced by First Nations' groups in what is now known as the United States. Those Aboriginal peoples learnt agriculture from the First Nations' people living in what is now Mexico, who were the first known peoples to cultivate corn.

Upon the arrival of the white man from Europe, entire Aboriginal civilizations were flourishing on our shores. They spoke many languages, but, tragically, many of them were killed or have died out. In the face of much persecution and devastation, they continued to practice their religion and maintain their cultural values. Today, although there has been a tremendous decline in the level of Native culture in Canada, parts of the country are experiencing a renaissance of First Nations' cultures and languages. This is particularly true in the Far North, specifically in Nunavut, and in the Prairie Provinces. There are now 1,172,790 Aboriginals living in Canada, and this statistic accounts for 3.8% of the Canadian population. Quite a number of First Nations' people reside in Scarborough.

The second wave of immigrants to Scarborough came from Europe almost 500 years ago. It is interesting to note that, on August 27, 1791, Lieutenant Governor John Graves Simcoe of Upper Canada officially named our region Scarborough.

Whenever I meet with Councilor Michael Thompson, attend the Lawrence Festival at Wexford and travel across Lawrence East, passing David and Mary Thompson Collegiate Institute, I always think of the Thompsons, the distinguished Scarborough pioneers who arrived here in the 1790s. We citizens of Scarborough are honored to have their names grace the school.

The Thompson and the other settlers of the time had very difficult lives. Nevertheless, they were steadfast in their determination to build up Scarborough, and, thanks to these tireless pioneers, Scarborough got off to a wonderful start. At that time the population density was very low, and the supply of land far greater than the demand for it. Incredibly, crown lands were sold at the rate of seventy-five cents per acre. Today an equivalent amount of land in Scarborough costs approximately half a million dollars or more.

When we look at Scarborough's burgeoning population today, it is hard to imagine that the area was not always so densely populated. According to the census of March 1809, in the Town of Scarborough there were 34 men, 24 women ands 82 children—a total of 140 souls. Today the average number of people living in a Scarborough high-rise is over one thousand. A few years prior to that census, in 1802, the number of inhabitants stood at only eighty-nine. Most of them were of British and French origin.

The economic depression of 1820-1850 brought Great Britain to its knees. Foreign trade collapsed. Small farms were sold to rich people and were turned into estates. The economic challenges of the time resulted in heavy job and property losses. Around the same time, the Irish Potato Famine hit Ireland very badly, and hundreds of thousands fled the country in order to survive. In addition, the Industrial Revolution eliminated the need for large numbers of workers, so a labor surplus developed. The unemployment rate skyrocketed as machinery replaced human labor. Meanwhile, the cost of living kept increasing but the minimum wage was brought down due to the labour surplus. All this adversity led to mass migration, and, indeed, the Government of Great Britain encouraged the exodus as they could see no way to support the population. Some of the emigrants settled in Scarborough, and their contributions to the town made it grow exponentially. It is remarkable that the population of Scarborough increased from 477 in 1820 to 1,135 in 1830.

At first, education was left to the settlers. The planning, collection of the necessary resources, establishing schools and funding were not institutionalized. Of course, at that time a basic education was not considered a fundamental right. It was not mandatory for the government of the day to provide an education for ordinary children.

In response to the protests of the people, the Legislature of Upper Canada accepted upon itself the responsibility of providing basic education. This policy was implemented in the Town of Scarborough towards the end of 1817. The first school was established at the Thompson-Springfield farm and was followed at the L'Amoureux settlement. Subsequently, additional schools were established in other parts of Scarborough.

At that time both birth rates and death rates were high, but the natural increase in population was quite low. Poor health care and high infant and adult mortality were the cause. Indeed, the mortality rate in certain areas was as high as 60% during the 1830s. Many settlers died of tuberculosis, malaria, cholera, typhoid, typhus and smallpox.

As time went on, great advances in health care were made, immigration increased and Scarborough began to move from its rural and agricultural roots to an urban and industrial environment. The wooden houses gradually disappeared and were replaced by houses made of sturdy brick.

As well, the development of roads and transportation brought much-needed prosperity to Scarborough. Along with bicycles, electric trains were introduced. The telephone opened up new pathways of business and social life. The automobile, as well, contributed a great deal to the development of Scarborough. Cars and buses filled the streets. All of this brought about a dramatic increase in population: At the beginning of the 20th century, the population of Scarborough stood at 11,746.

While World War I left Canada with devastating losses, Canadians were proud that their efforts had contributed to the Allied victory in Europe. The advent of World War II, however, shook North America, Europe and much of the rest of the world to its very roots. After the war ended in 1945, our soldiers returned home and settled down. Family life flourished, and the so-called baby boomers, along with many refugees and immigrants, made a very positive impact on the demographic pattern.

Since those days, Scarborough has become home to a multitude of newcomers who have brought their rich cultures, age-old languages, deeply held heritage values, special traditions, outstanding skills, long years of experience and many other assets to our community. Many of them also brought with them the suffering they experienced as a result of torture, genocide, discrimination and persecution. Others arrived as victims of natural calamities such as floods, tsunamis, volcanic eruption and drought. Others, however, came here with the resources to invest abundant capital in our community, and life in Scarborough has flourished as a result.

Scarborough is full of highly skilled people and outstanding professionals. Workers in the business and manufacturing sectors also contribute to the vibrant social climate in our community today. Scarborough is filled with positive energy, and artistic and cultural festivals fill our streets throughout the year. People here generally live together in peace and harmony, and they care for one another. They share their values, and, together, are quietly building up a very positive community heritage.

There are, of course, some negative aspects to life in our community. Tragically, youth violence, dysfunctional families, theft, vandalism, the drug trade and homelessness affect growing cities all over the world. Scarborough is no exception, but countless good-hearted people in the political, social, educational, religious, medical and business sectors are working hard to eliminate these problems. Results of these initiatives can already be seen, and their efforts will continue to bear fruit.

In conclusion, Scarborough is a city of old, established families and the newcomers who have joined them in creating a vibrant, progressive society. Scarborough is not at the bottom of the heap; it is a wonderful and thriving city. Newcomers are welcome to join us, and so are visitors. Please come to Scarborough and enjoy all that our community has to offer. You will not be disappointed.

CHAPTER THIRTEEN

NOTHERNERS TO BE FREE AND STRONG

I had the privilege in attending the last campaign meeting of the parliamentary election in the GTA on October 2008 with Steven Harper. Harper, in his elegant speech, used the expression' the true north strong and free' when he referred to the protection of northern Canada inclusive of the ocean boundaries, from aggressive neighboring counties It opened my deeply buried concerns regarding the North and prompted me to write this article.

The magnetic true north in the northern hemisphere is slightly west of the designated north pole at 90 degrees north longitude and is inclined towards Canadian territory. Our northern region has to be free from other Northern nations and be seriously protected; it is now free from air, water and noise pollution, though the effects of Global warming are present. The north is, for the most part, free from crime, not overburdened with a large population and is free from the usual hustle and bustle that we Southerners have come to view as normal.

Those I refer to as "Northerners' are addressed by other terms such as the Natives, Native Indians, Aboriginals, and more commonly, the First Nations and in the rest of my article I shall address them as the First Nations. Although all human beings are related and referred to as higher animals in biology and form one species, some are more alike and others are less alike in physical appearance, customs, traditions, food habits, systems of marriage, languages, and ways of living have determined the differences between different ethnic groups.

In a micro-analysis, there are 58 foundation groups belonging to the First Nations culture. I use the word culture because many First

Nations people do not like to be labeled an "ethnic group" and thus "culture" is a more respectful term.

The First Nations peoples were the first inhabitants of the so called new world. The reason I say the so-called new word is because East and Southeast Asians arrived in central, south and southern parts of North America by navigating over the Pacific Ocean over a thousand years ago. But the arrival of the First Nations was not by navigation, but on foot. It has been accepted by anthropologists and archaeologists that the First Nations arrived as the first human beings from Asia, via the Bering Strait. Although, the origin and the date of arrival of these first inhabitants cannot be determined, the most accepted theory, commonly referred to as the "Coastal Migration Theory" is that the First Nations arrived from Asia between 35, 000-50,000 years ago via the land bridge known as 'Beringia'. Their pedestrian land route began on the North American west coast and ended at the southernmost tip of South America.

It is a historical accident that the word Indian is used to denote this group of people. The origins of these people have been a mystery for a very long time. There has, and still continues to be a lot of research done by historians and archeologists. The evidence that has been found is fascinating, but some is very contradictory. Most of the native groups have their own stories and traditions as to their origins and they are indeed glorious and beautiful. But they are not scientifically or objectively collected and reported.

Some old records say that the Natives were refugees from the Garden of Eden, driven out after the fall. Others thought that the Natives were the descendants of people carried on the Ark built by Noah. There is another popular explanation that appears to have originated with a Dutch man named Fredericus Lumnius in the 1560s. He noticed that there were many similarities between the ten tribes of Israel (the so called "lost tribes") with American natives. (Old Testament, 2 Kings 17.6).

There is another idea that the Natives have similarities with the inhabitants of the lost continent of Atlantis. There is another theory the natives had come from the ancient Phoenician culture or later from the Welsh settlers led by Prince Modoc in the twelfth century.

In 1589, Father Jose de Acosta pointed out in his <u>Historia Naturaly Moral de Las Indias</u> that the native inhabitants of America had Asiatic origins.

The biblical concept of the origin of man somehow got limited to the scientific outcome. Those who believe in the theory that man was created by God as Adam and Eve would not accept that man originated from the zanthanarpous an advanced species of monkey which is promoted in the evolutionary theory of Darwin. Further evidence provided by archaeologists, who excavated the ruins and remains of aboriginals brought facts. Historians like William Prescott were able to piece together information about conquered civilizations through evidence. It was not in a written form. They usually obtained artifacts such as pots, human skulls, stones, hair, coins and other belongings. The early archaeologists uncovered pictographs and hieroglyphs from the Mayan civilization in the Yucatan peninsula in Mexico in the middle of the nineteenth century. It became increasingly clear that there were no ancient caves or old tools to be found at the bottom of glacial deposits that would provide evidence of the origins of the North American native people. I believe sufficient interest would have led to finding more archaeological evidence.

The discovery of a spear point buried inside an extinct animal in 1908 near Folsom, New Mexico led to further excavation near Folsom in 1926 which turned up evidence of human occupation that went back at least 10,000 years. All other research proved that human habitation was somewhere in the same period of time.

The number of languages that these people spoke was over 2,200 and did not originate from a mono culture and was based on many complex and high degrees of diverse linguistic families. The linguistic development was very limited and slow and hardly had any written scripts. These were oral cultures and the people passed on their experiences, medical knowledge, songs, stories, and ceremonies from one generation to the next in this way. Verbal communication was sufficient because their communication circle was small, limited to families and small settlements. Later on, when larger settlements were formed and agriculture developed, the circle was extended, and the need for better communication arose.

Nature blessed the land with costly minerals and resources, such as diamonds, natural gas and untapped oil. The size of the Northwest Territories is 3, 426,320 Sq kilometers. This is ten times the size of Great Britain and covers 34% of the total Canadian land mass. The newly created territory of Nunavut was created from the central and eastern parts of the Northwest Territories. Nunavut was officially proclaimed in July 1993 in recognition of the heritage and values of the Inuit who account for 85% of its population. This territory has the size of almost two million sq kilometers and covers one fifth of Canadian land. The Yukon is another wonderful territory where the First Nations mainly occupy. The southern boarder of the northern region is marked as 60 degrees latitude north and has a small temperate climatic zone and the rest is a cold desert region.

The main overall factor that governs the life of northerners is the elements, the extreme cold climate and seasons, not the government. It was once said that the sun never set in the former British Empire. But in northern Canada, the sun never sets for months in the summer and in the winter; the land is in perpetual darkness. The cool, fresh air, frozen rivers and lakes surrounded by thinly populated villages and towns, wild animals and the beloved domestic animals moving around with family members like skin on the body, greetings with warmth and deep rooted affection even to strangers and the kind hospitality is a fabulous image in and of itself.

We also should give due consideration to the fight against unsuitable climatic conditions that Canadians living in the polar region (66.5-90 latitude) face. Whenever we watch the weather forecast on television, particularly in the winter, at times it would say that the day's temperature is – 20 degrees and with the wind shield from the northern winds is -35 degrees. I wonder how the northerners fight against these temperatures even though they are accustomed to it. Still, they are not polar bears who are naturally protected by God. With all these unfavorable conditions, the Natives could do better if the rest of Canada takes their developments more seriously and the Natives make serous commitments.

Historically speaking, the size, density and the rate of increase in population amongst the First Nations was very low. Although there was a high birth rate, infant mortality, lack of medical facilities, diet, lack of education and natural calamities reduced the size of the population. Then, during the era of discovery and colonization, the Europeans eliminated countless numbers of natives in roughly 500 years. The First Nations settled in Canada during the Stone Age with bows and arrows and slowly improvised their tools and improved their way of living over the course of time. But the Europeans, migrated at an advanced stage of the pre industrial era with guns and sophisticated weapons of the time. They also brought with them diseases such as smallpox. The Europeans in Canada still maintained their relationship with their ancestors but the natives had lost their ancestral connections and thus became totally committed to this land. North, Central and South America are the only home these people know and have connections with.

Many of these people claim that the Europeans invaded, took their land and forcibly resettled them on unsuitable land we now refer to as Reserves. The First Nations people account for almost 2% of the population and they have some special rights accorded to them because of government Treaties. Their situation is quite different from the rest of Canadians. They have been addressed like Quebec as a nation but their demographic distribution is not confined to particular areas. Therefore their rights, responsibilities, and modernization plans have to be based on their values and way of life. It is absurd to say that most of them are lazy, habitually enslaved to alcohol, not interested in attending schools, not willing to participate in the rest of Canadian society and make their lives more productive. Though we have a duty and responsibility to correct historical wrongs and assist the First Nations people, they should show their goodwill as well. It is not a one way tariff to claim that you took our land therefore you have to look after us. They should not remain in the past when the world is changing so quickly. The conditions and the development that the northerners have to make will not only improve their conditions, but also develop all of Canada.

Canada is a diverse nation in many respects and the federal government is obligated to take of every political unit be it a province or territory. It is clear that there is an imbalance in many areas such as the location of natural resources, education, technology, health care facilities, demographic distribution, political awareness, social developments, economic strength, transportation and communication in all of the provinces and territories. Economically they can be classified into 2 main groups, the have and have not provinces and territories. Bear in mind that this demarcation has changed as evidenced by the recent discovery and development of crude oil resources in Newfoundland. Newfoundland is now considered a "have" province. On the other hand, Ontario is on the verge of dropping down to the have not status, if adequate measures are not taken by both the provincial and federal government. The initiative made by Dalton McGuinty, the Premier of Ontario regarding equalization payments calls for the creation of a better formula so that the so called "have" provinces can obtain a better share of the national pie. But the obligation of the federal government is to treat all provinces and territories , according to their needs and concerns , considering all are children of the same parents and at times it may give more to the weaker ones.

The First Nations have some long standing grievances. Some have been attended to by the government and the outcomes have not been very satisfying because they did not resolve any of the fundamental issues. These issues are of serious concern to all of us and must be resolved for any healing to take place. Many First Nations feel that they are partially isolated, in many aspects of Canadian life, and many mainstream Canadians believe that the First Nations people need to solve this problem on their own. But there is an element of truth in this and we all have to make an effort and bridge the gap gradually and let the First Nations people know that they are valued and respected. There is a pressing need for having better interaction and by sharing common values and understanding each other, it will clear up certain attitudes and misunderstandings.

Among many other issues, land claims are a major one. Oka/ Kanasetake, Gustaffson Lake, and Ipperwash are a few notable examples. Ipperwash is particularly special in that an unarmed Native protestor, Dudley George was shot and killed. This terrible incident sparked a 10 year push for a public inquiry which finally took place in 2005. Anyone measuring the size of their land compared with the rest of Canada may arrive at the wrong conclusion that the Native people occupy a major portion of the land, but in the actual sense it is not true, Although the Native people were pushed off most of the easily inhabitable, and arable land, this is a sensitive issue because of their spiritual and cultural attachments to the land and the sentiment cannot be gauged and presented in numbers or degrees. In spite of the historical disputes, a negotiable settlement can be made. The Nis'ga Treaty is one such example. Though it is a complex and complicated issue, it is not an impossible task to be resolved. There is no scarcity of land for Canadians, in fact Canada can easily accommodate the same size of population in addition to the current population and flourish. It is important for the Canadian government to resolve the outstanding land claims and respect the First Nations' right to self government.

The second important factor is inadequate infrastructure. On many reserves, especially in the North the people live in what could be described as Third World conditions. In some of these places, there is no running water, no dependable transportation and no adequate hospitals even though abundant hydro electric resources are available. We should not forget that federal government grants of any kind are greater for people compared with the population, but there is another factor that we have to take into consideration. This sparsely populated region demands more allocation of capital and concurrent expenditure. The First Nations people who live in these areas have every right to modern conveniences and comforts.

Many other concerns for First Nations people can be addressed by expanding educational facilities. Modern education and technology has brought revolutionary change in all aspects of human life around the world. First of all, all native parents and children must develop a trust in that modern education is universal. It is not the white man's treasure. I am certain that many educated First Nations people understand my point here. In fact, under the Universal Declaration of the United Nations, education is a fundamental right of a child and it is the responsibility of the government to provide it. The Canadian government acts accordingly, but the enrolment rate is lagging behind. The drop out rate is also high in some provinces and territories as well. The completion of high school will not only facilitate in finding better employment, but it is also an important tool in terms of knowing their rights and duties in Canadian society Education also helps in the integration process, while preserving their age old values. Our education system can easily accommodate these values.

The initiatives made by the Christian missionaries in the education of First Nations children, was originally to educate them and bring them up to the modern world with a slight injection and indulgence of their faith Most of the Christian missionaries began with providing humanitarian services without expecting any return, but later on the colonial masters realized that getting faithful support from the people through religious conversion would be easy and strong.

The way the residential schools functioned eventually deviated from its original purpose. Some of the First Nations students were terribly abused in an attempt to destroy any pride in their culture. Though it is hard to determine the extent of the abuse, there is evidence that this occurred and we as Canadian must not overlook this part of our history. I thank Mr. Steven Harper for making an apology in parliament and the full support extended by the members of parliament without any reservation. In spite of this, education is the basic right of these children and it is the responsibility of governments and parents to educate them without giving any lame excuses and if the students do not attend school, the parents also have to share the blame. Unlike other countries where children cannot go to school because of poverty, or due to the use of child labour, in Canada there is no excuse for children not to attend school. The social amenities of the welfare state are very unique in providing basic needs, and if anyone misuses or allocates support in a wrong direction, the government should not be blamed.

The written history of Canada and the school curriculum are very open and fair for the most part, but the subject of pre European history has to be more balanced.

Economic development and better employment facilities are another main concern. There are better employment prospects in the North due to the development of natural resources. The expansions of hydro electricity, investing in the mining industry are some examples. Modernizing the tourism industry, encouraging the development of winter sports and so on will make our north sound.

There is no Berlin Wall in Canada that has to be demolished. The Northerners take imitative to come down south and closely intermingle and make their lives happy while the rest of us should warmly welcome and be partners in sharing this life with them. There are wonderful places for us to visit and learn more about fellow Canadians. The Government has a fiduciary relationship with the First Nations and this relationship must be respected. The Gomery Commission is providing an opportunity for many First Nations people to tell their stories and it is up to each and every one of us to listen with an open heart.

CHAPTER FOURTEEN

ELECTION TORCH 2007
VOTER TRUNS CANDIDATE

It was a very pleasant and warm afternoon in the middle of a beautiful summer at about 3.pm at the Scarborough Civic Centre. The Centre was filled with enthusiastic and politically motivated members of the Scarborough Centre Riding Association and hundreds lined up in front of the council chamber mainly in support of myself (Samy Appadurai) in my nomination as a candidate in the forth coming provincial election, and to take part in the Annual General Meeting. At one outstanding point, both of the candidates who had campaigned against me gave me their whole hearted support and I was unanimously chosen to be the candidate for Scarborough Centre.

In my acceptance speech, I clearly stated that the " election process is part of the entire political process like the waterfall is part of a river but the overall political responsibilities and participation is a flowing river from the upper course through the middle course till the lower course. Therefore, let us keep up the enthusiasm, support and good work, so that we shall overcome the current challenges and keep our Ontario on the top of the Canadian map and our great nation Canada on the top of the globe. I being an Ontarian, visualize the progress of Canada through Ontario. It is also our moral obligation to remember our forefathers at this moment and thank them for building this nation at the time of absence of modern technology with the help of hand tools. This nation in a virgin forest, with all sorts of hardship and suffering handed to us a developed, rich nation with peace and harmony, and we all enjoy the fruits. It does not end here, we have to hand it over to the next generation without passing any burdens such as more government debt and deteriorated social amenities and so on….." I am very proud to say that my long speech was well received and brought many new members closer to the party and affirmed commitment in the election campaign.

As businessmen value customer satisfaction, politicians put the well being of the people as their top priority. The only difference between the two is that our concerns go beyond the Election Day and in most cases conclude at the end of a political term though not always. Most of the politicians in the three levels of government commit to do their best for the people, irrespective of their own victory or defeat in the election. Election to public office does not mean the beginning of a public life or the start of a political career. It is only a milestone on the journey and one of the means in carrying out public policies. Using other means and available resources along with participating in the evolving political exercise also comes into play. I have been involved in politics ever since I was a high school student and when I worked on a contract basis in Nigeria and Ethiopia in the field of education. The restrictions placed on foreigners limited our involvement in politics. That being said however, politics is not an area that can be kept in a water tight compartment. It is an essential part of life integrated with education, the economy, social norms of society and so on. I was very encouraged in voicing my views on anti apartheid and some other areas of common concern for Africans. I was able to make an impact because I could speak their languages and closely intermingled with the people at the grass roots level. In one of the meetings, someone in the crowd branded me as an agent of the CIA and I went through a hard time for this mere baseless guess that spread like wild fire until it was cleared. Blindly following a leader and acting accordingly, without giving any independent thought is pretty common. The interesting part of it is that when a leader is in power, he is considered to be almost divine even though he may be a crook. At one time in history, the British kings were thought to never make any mistakes and whatever they did was never questioned because of the view of "Divine Right". But today, the Monarchy is symbolic and has no real power. When a politician is deposed or removed from power, he will be portrayed as incompetent and all of his wrongdoings will be out on display.

I appreciate the maturity of the Americans in judging political issues. A good example is Richard Nixon who was removed for his involvement in the Watergate scandal of 1974. A few years later when a critical issue on the Middle East conflict arose, he was invited with respect, to share his expertise and experience. I admire the Canadian politicians on occasions when they crossed party lines and worked together for the national interest. When Mr. John Charest, the federal leader of the Progressive Conservative Party moved into the position of the provincial Liberal leader in Quebec, this move helped maintain national unity. But I do not admire the coalition formed in 2008 by the Liberals and NDP during a global economic tsunami. This move was made to capitalize on the unstable economic condition of Canada in order to change the government.

Here, the actions made by politicians either reflect the people's attitudes and views or is an attempt to impose their views and desires by presenting their agenda in a sugar coated pill. I do not under estimate the intelligence of Canadians. For example in most cases, Canadians have elected the political party that can rule the country and face the challenges and find better solutions to meet them. But in some cases, emotion motivated the course of the voting and focus. Canadians are smart like the British. When Britain was seriously involved as a part of the alliance in the Second World War against Germany, Japan and Italy, they elected Mr. Adley as the Prime Minister who was capable and able to handle the situation well and as the British people expected, did a marvelous job. Just after the war, during the early days of peace the British people noticed that there were other leaders who could handle the new situation better and failed to re elect him as the Prime Minister.

Let me come back to the experiences that I gained in my election campaign. My campaign manager, David is a very patriotic Canadian. He is well balanced, rational and very conservative in managing the finances, riding association members and my beloved volunteers who had foregone their personal benefit and concerns and worked for me day and night. During the summer months the campaign manager and I visited a couple of houses just to get to know the primary concerns and pressing needs from the public directly. We noticed on several occasions that a reasonable number of the houses we approached were temporarily occupied by the friends and relatives of the homeowners who had left for vacation either within Canada or outside. In a way, this provided an opportunity to explore their concerns in their respective provinces and compare them with ours. This was okay for familiarization visits but not for the election campaign because of the fact that these same streets may have to be revisited later on. Traveling long distances and meeting fewer voters during the summer proved to be a real challenge. The timing was another main factor that determined the marginal utility of our efforts very significantly. Usually voters make their decision during the last weekend before the election and until then they are engaged with many other affairs. They keep on listening to the debates among the candidates, comparing the strength and skills of the party leaders and polices before finally deciding for whom they are going to cast their vote.

Normally, one of the most important factors that boost the popular vote is the party leadership. Once the voters determine that the leader has the leadership qualities, educational background, experience, confidence, and capacities coupled with instant decision making power and honesty, then they will cast their ballot accordingly. The strength of the party at times rises due to smart leadership; on the contrary a well established party may lose the popular vote and strength mainly because of inadequate leadership qualities. This appears to be evident in the last parliamentary election on 14th October 2008 where the Liberal party leader Stephan Dion was blamed for the lowest voter turnout ever earned by the party. Though Jack Layton's leftist polices were not much appreciated by the general masses, his leadership qualities were accounted in the public polls as second to P.M Stephen Harper. Right or wrong, he presented his policies in a very commanding and convincing manner. Of course P.M Steven Harper had governed firmly and for a longer period than any other minority government and cleverly implemented many of his election promises in a short period of time which allowed him to be voted in for a second term of office.

People generally look into the party and its policies and compare and decide to vote for the one that has more benefit to them. One example is the issue of increasing or levying new taxes either directly or indirectly. When it comes to the impact of tax reduction, in some cases most people are able to realize fully the benefits that arise from tax reduction. For example, the Conservative Government of Ontario under Premier Mike Harris, reduced the personal income tax amount substantially and employees began to take home more money in every pay cheque. The impact was not felt all at once because it was implemented slowly; whereas the 2006 Child Care Benefit of one hundred dollars per child for low income families implemented by the Federal government, made many parents happy very quickly. Quite a large number of people expressed their grievances towards Ontario Premier Dalton McGuinty when he levied the health care premium, a regressive tax, after promising not to increase taxes. The public's disappointment was visible at the beginning of the election campaign, but later on the people were concerned with other issues and it did not become a major deciding factor and lost its weight in the election.

Other ways of balancing the budget or avoiding heavy deficits is to reduce social services such as closing some schools, hospitals, and other social amenities. This will also bring down the popularity of the government. It is as bad as increasing taxes, but the only difference is that the taxes are levied for all, based either in the form of progressive or proportional formulas. Not everyone consistently and equally makes use of the services provided by hospital and schools. People are very concerned about the promises made by their politicians before the election and how well they keep these promises and implement them once elected. There are politicians who knowingly make promises up to the sky and deliberately do not keep, nor did they intend to. For example, when Jean Chrétien was campaigning against Brian Mulroney, the most attractive campaign promise was to remove the G.S.T. But after three consecutive terms of office— he did not do this. Another example is in Ontario when Dalton McGuinty while canvassing for the 2004 election made many promises that he knew he could not keep. Some politicians make promises to the voters that are genuine, but do to the circumstances after the election are not able to fulfill them. A current example of this deals with the Federal Deficit. It was initially promised by the Federal government that there would not be a deficit. But due to the global economic downturn, it was impossible not to run a deficit.

Looking back on this experience, I realize that this journey is one of amazing twists and turns. Wherever I went on this road, I encountered and interacted with many people from many walks of life. Over the course of time, I became increasingly closer to the people, not as a politician, but as a human being; their issues were my issues and their causes were also my own. Instead of seeing divisions, I saw an opportunity to engage the public and serve the people.

CHAPTER FIFTEEN

CANADIAN CULTURAL MOSAIC

George W. Bush, the former U.S President of the United States of America visited the American coalition forces along with the American troops and other personnel in Iraq to bid them farewell, before handing over the presidency to Barack Obama. He also took the time to thank the Iraqi authorities and government officials who supported him in his fight against terrorism. While having a press conference, an Iraqi journalist removed his pair of shoes, aimed them at Mr. Bush's face and threw them. It became a very sensitive issue and spread like a wild fire in the media around the world. Neither the Bush administration nor the western world could comprehend the seriousness and the depth of this gesture. The Arab world and South East Asians viewed Mr. Bush's visit as an insult and the shoe throwing incident magnified this point. Some westerners might have expressed their disappointment, disagreement or anger by throwing rotten eggs at his face. Whatever the weapon of choice, the point was clear.

I would also like to cite another incident that happened in Uganda. The former president of Uganda Mr. Milton Obeto travelled to Singapore to attend the British Commonwealth Summit in 1971. Mr. Idi Amin, a high ranking army officer who was originally employed as a cook in the British Army toppled Obeto's government in a coup d'etat. On one occasion he wanted to insult Mr. Obeto and addressed him as a "woman". In our culture, this would mean nothing to us but in their culture it is the ultimate insult for a man.

The culture of a particular ethnic group has certain positive or negative values and strengths but to outsiders it means absolutely nothing. Every one of us belongs to a particular ethnic group and is bound to be influenced by its culture. Culture is multidimensional. It begins from the private life of an individual, extends to the family circle and then to the public life of the ethnic group. I can cite numerous examples from the simple to the complex to illustrate this point. For example, bodily contact in greeting in the East and South East Asian cultures is very limited especially between members of the opposite sex from teenagers to seniors. Orthodox Jews avoid bodily contact with the opposite sex while greeting each other. In the Italian, French, Greek, Portuguese, Spanish and Ethiopian Orthodox Christian cultures, kissing on both the cheeks is an accepted and welcomed way of greeting. Dress code is also very interesting in many cultures. When the singer Janet Jackson was performing in a concert, a portion of her upper dress was torn off, exposing one of her breasts. This became a big issue and she lost a wonderful chance in performing a prestigious show. In contrast to this, I visited an ethnic group in Sokoto state, Nigeria and saw that from small girls to older women, even ones who were educated in the west were topless in public and this was considered an honourable way to preserve their culture. However, in some other part of the same state breastfeeding a baby in a public place was not accepted. Shaking hands has become common among people of the same sex in the urban areas in Asia whereas in other cultures there is a formula of hand shaking. For the Yoruba of Nigeria it is expected that the man of greater status, age or power initiates the hand shake and the other party responds. When I was working in Nigeria, at the initial stage when I met anyone in meetings and public gatherings irrespective of his or her status I extended my hand to shake equally. Later on I came to know that extending hands to high ranking traditional rulers and governing officers before allowing them to extend their hand first was an insult. If the official extended his hand to you to shake, it was considered an honour. I was told that I had to know the status of the people and greet them accordingly. Some cultural interpretation of other hand gestures might have opposite meanings. In another case, for an example in Afghanistan and some other Asian cultures the thumps-up sign has a sexual connotation as the Canadian middle finger gesture. One of the common cultural shocks between new immigrants of certain ethnic groups with the Canadian mainstream is the issue of eye contact. In mainstream Canadian culture, maintaining eye contact is a must while having business or private conversations but to ethnic groups from countries such as South American, Caribbean, most of Africa and Asia eye contact is initially avoided. For many of these cultures, direct eye contact with women can be very uncomfortable as it seen as disrespectful to look into the eyes of a woman who is not ones spouse or relative.

There are numerous definitions of culture by anthropologists, historians, sociologists, religious groups and linguistics scholars. In general, the culture of an ethnic group is a product of multiple strains and it is a system of ideals and ideas that cultivate behaviors and a pattern of life of a group of people which is then passed on from generation to generation. It is also a product of natural instinct. The interesting part of it is that every human being is unique and even identical twins born by the same parents have differences in terms of their bodies, mind and emotions. But human wants and basic needs are very much identical and in some cases they are the same in when we consider fundamental needs such as food for hunger, sleep for rest, sex for pleasure and so on. The goals of living for every one of us irrespective of religion color, ethnicity, educational background, or socio-economic status is to be happy and I am very certain that no one will disagree on this point. But the means of obtaining happiness, even the meaning of happiness itself certainly varies from one to another. Culture consists of many ingredients such as food habits, manners, greetings, clothing, festivals and celebrations, games, etiquette between superiors and elders, feasts, marriage, family relationship, relations between husband and wife, parents and children, families and so on. Let us also not forget the cultural influence on the arts and the political system as well. The proportion of the composition varies between different groups. The Islamic Arab culture for example is more centered on their religious beliefs whereas in other cultures, religion may not play such an integral role. Culture is also not static and it is constantly under going changes. Due to the influence of various contributing factors a culture periodically acquires a new shape. The British culture of the Elizabethan era and pre and post Industrial Revolution underwent some fundamental changes from the royal family to the gross roots level. In China Mao Tse Tung brought a cultural revolution in China which brought the Chinese in line with communist ideology and attempted to do away with the past. After Mao's death, the impact of the Communist and Cultural Revolutions dwindled in some areas but was strengthened in others and we still see its influence today.

Ecology is one of the chief factors that have molded many cultures around the world. It covers mainly the physical environment such as climate, physical features and the location of the region. The natural climate of the coastal regions differs from the land locked regions. Mountains, plateaus, deserts and other climatic zones have had an influence in the evolution of many cultures. One interesting influence of the environment in culture is the impact on languages. For example, in the Canadian Arctic, due to climate change many foreign species of insects are now being noted. But the Inuit people do not have words in their language for these species; they now have to invent words.

Historical events also make an impact in the cultural patterns of an ethnic group. The systematic wipe out of the Jews by Nazi rule and anti Zionist governments have made the Jews more ethnic centered than ever before. The colonization of Africa by the European empires brought many small kingdoms together and formed a nation to an extent. But when independence was granted or won by armed uprising, the colonial rulers demarked arbitrary boundaries which whether deliberately or not, split the various ethnic populations which in turn caused cultural upheaval, political instability and ethnic conflict. In South Africa under the apartheid regime, the whites of Germany, Britain, Holland and other European nations viewed themselves as the superior race. Due to their common interest and intermingling they created a new white ethnicity and called themselves Afrikaners. The Métis in Canada and some ethnic groups in South America are the products of inter ethnic relationships and marriages; respectively the Europeans and natives in Canada and Blacks with Spanish in South America. But similar intermarriages between the natives and Europeans in the rest of America did not have much impact.

Religious faith is another factor that influences the culture of the followers. At the early stages in Canada the Roman Catholic and other Christian denominations were part of the government and influenced their culture by having their religious input in the formation of their culture and later on the separation of the Church from the government reduced its influence in both the pubic and private spheres. But the revival of the Islamic faith in these days has a very high influence in various ethnic groups and their culture is shifting from an ethnic centered one to a faith centered one.

The technological revolution has made big changes in the cultural pattern of the human race all over the world. Technological development brought many people from the rural areas into the urban centres and the concentration of people and the density of population reached very high levels. People migrated from many ethnic groups to urban areas where mass production provided an improved standard of living. The abundant opportunities in making use of their extra time along with a steady income assisted them in planning for the future, enriched educational skills, provided job security rather than seasonal work and generally allowed for the greater exchange of ideas and values. Urbanization also allowed for the expansion of ones social circle outside the family to include not just colleagues but also friends and other members of the community.

The penetration of the technological culture into the rural is expanding and technology has a strong impact on culture. Globalization is a silent evolutionary process shared by everyone but in different ways reaching a higher degree of adaptation. The interesting part of it is that it has become a universal culture, and the main characteristics are common or similar in cities from New York to Tokyo. But it is foreign concept in the hinterlands in there own areas. Since it is very rampant in the western world and America, it is labeled as "western culture" or "American culture" or "modern culture" but in the actual sense it is a by product of modern technology.

Immigration is the other dynamic factor that makes fundamental changes in many ethnic groups who migrate to other nations. Both internal and external immigration is due to the lack of human resources in an advanced economy and the decline in birth rate. This leads to a situation in which there are not enough people to take up certain economic positions. In Canada the need for skilled workers has been an increasing trend. At the initial stage, immigrants came from a handful of traditional countries such as France and the United Kingdom. There was a continuous link between the sending and receiving countries and cultural integration was not a major issue. When economic development reached a high level, the demand for the human resources increased and the migration rate declined. But in Canada the growth of the economy in the waste land containing abundant minerals increased the demand for more new immigrants. Once there was a decline in the migration rate from France and the United Kingdom, Canada had to find alternative sources and encouraged migration from the Southern and Eastern European nations. Although they had their own cultural differences, there were enough common elements in their lifestyle and their cultural and ecological similarities. It was not hard for these new immigrants to become integrated with the Canadian mainstream as opposed to current times. Since 1960, the direction was changed and the immigration gates were widely opened to Asia, Africa and South America.

Canada as the highest per capita immigration rate in the world and almost 20% of the Canadian population were born in foreign countries and migrated to Canada. Most of the recent new immigrants in particular have come with their rich culture, fine arts, skills and education and these are an asset to us, not liabilities. However, there are a few elements who have come with their home country problems and that may appear uncomfortable to others. But this does not appear to pollute the Canadian atmosphere. As is often the case, new immigrants at the initial stage find it extremely hard to move on from where they once were. Most them had well paying jobs job, good position, were well respected and had recognition but when they arrived in Canada the reality hit very hard. Many new immigrants struggle due to culture shock, lack of official language skills, lack of labour market knowledge and the economy. This stage is temporary but not easy to pass through and can be humiliating and frustrating. That being said however many new immigrants have turned these blocking stones into stepping stones.

Once they reestablish their life they join up with the vertical mosaic group. These high ranking white collar job holders form a new group of interests and their caliber gets into their orbit from their ethnic cultural dominating influences. They share their feelings with their new group, lead their life in a sophisticated manner and go into the orbit of other planets with people of the same caliber but belonging to many other ethnic groups.

Another group of newcomers become absorbed by territorial groups who came earlier and settled down in farming communities in the west. They arrived from their respective countries to a place where the farms were larger in size and the settlements were scattered. The density of population is thinner and mostly confirmed within a circle containing the flavour of their mono cultural environment. Some of them continued their life as was in their homeland; meeting with their group of people on the farms, shops, schools and public functions, reading their newspapers and listen their community radio programs. They hardly intermingled with dominate ethnic groups. These settlements were found mostly in Saskatchewan, Alberta and Manitoba. They brought their culture and also maintained their individual languages.

In some instances within the same ethnic group itself because of differences in economic and educational achievements, there are groups that split off and do not maintain close interactions with the main group even though they share the same linguistic, cultural and ethnic values. For example, the Chinese and Sikhs who arrived over one hundred years ago as unskilled temporary foreign workers to build the Canadian Pacific Railway gradually got settled themselves and led a modest life. But in the early 1990s when Hong Kong was to be handed back to mainland China by the British, many Chinese investors migrated in the investor's category of immigration and they were given a red carpet welcome by Canada and other developed nations. They preferred to associate closer with other entrepreneurs, irrespective of their ethnicity but not closely with the Chinese who were the second or third generation of the Chinese who came as workers.

The high impact of recent new immigrants was felt more in Ontario. In Ontario most of the new comers got themselves engaged in the service industry and manufacturing sectors. They are multi cultural but unilingual in nature. Their second and third generation is generally more inclined to accept the lifestyle of the mainstream. The linguistic skills in their heritage language and the attempts to learn are very limited. Not more than 30% of them attend heritage language classes and those who attend operate on very functional level.

In terms of cultural symbols, it easier to identify visible minorities, however some symbols can be ambiguous. A woman who wears a scarf over her head might be a Muslim; but she might be an Orthodox Christian, Jew or even a nun! But you cannot tell at least not visually if a person is Scottish, French or Swedish. Cultural symbols can be an object of great pride as well. For example, most of the Arab sheiks are very particular in exposing their identity through their dressing habits by wearing turbans on their heads while they are discharging their duties. They are successful in uniformed employment such as police officers and taxi drivers. I witnessed and took part in the Caribbean Celebration of 2007 in Toronto as a member of the Progressive Conservative party of Ontario. It was a wonderful celebration of Caribbean cultural dance and music particularly the blended black culture of the new continent Any one who has not had detailed knowledge of African culture and fine arts might have arrived at the conclusion that the exhibited cultural events are the true culture of the black race. Since I had been residing in Africa over 18 years, and intermingled with many ethnic groups and was a patron of the drama and music society of the Jimma Teachers College, I am aware that there are thousands of types of fine arts, music, and dances. It is not only the exhibited performances, it is a mixture.

In terms of the Canadian experience, the province of Quebec prefers to have a unilingual nature though they are a multicultural society. New Brunswick is a unique province where in the provincial level, the bilingual and multicultural function has been in existence. Multicultural and ethno-specific cultural festivals that are mainly organized by first generation immigrants with the support and participation by the second and third generation are more of a symbolic exercise. I have watched many such celebrations in the Portuguese, Greek, Indian, and Irish communities. I have also participated in numerous Tamil functions as a guest and at caravan festivals that embraced many cultural shows. They have a noble cause in preserving, promoting and having aesthetic pleasure but in the actual sense, it does not penetrate into their day to day life. The core of the culture is a way of living with their traditional values that have been cultivated, refined, preserved and proudly handed to this generation. The peer pressure from the dominant culture and the life pattern certainly has a strong influence. As someone's growth is very much influenced by the ecology, already well established the culture of the Anglophone and French culture continue to have its impact on the newcomers and it becomes natural phenomena and the resistance made by the ethnic group slowly disappears in the due course of time. Though the absolute freedom is given to practice one's culture, in practice it would not be possible as it appears in the Multiculturalism Act. There are two official languages declared but none of the cultures has been given the status of the national culture and Canada is a bilingual not bicultural nation. No culture is favoured and all are equally treated in the eyes of the law. It is left to the cultural groups themselves to preserve their culture and passing it on to the next generation.

In America, nationalism and statehood have taken the utmost priority. There is no question about German American, Irish American, Native Indian, Latino American, Asian American and African American heritage. No matter where your roots are, you are an American. That's it. Be a full fledge American or be a foreigner. There is no question of the coexistence of many ethnic groups. There is no mid-way.

In truth, there are no homogenous cultures in any nation on the globe. The national boundaries have been altered from time to time. Nations have been merged, separated and so on. There are non Jews in Israel and non Catholics in the Vatican and non Muslims in Saudi Arabia. Their numbers may be insignificant but there is no restriction by their constitution for other ethnic or religious people to be there. Even within the First Nations there are a lot of tribal groups that have been in existence. Though the Americans claim the Native Indians are part of the full fledge American culture, the native people do not totally agree. Some of the natives have the very strong conviction that Columbus did not discover America, rather he invaded it.

There is another aspect that is very interesting. The blacks who were brought from Africa as slaves and the (east) Indians and the Chinese as indentured workers were addressed as coolies, a word that might have origins in the Tamil language that is spoken mainly in South India and Sri Lanka, meaning labourer. Though they came from different tribes their categories of work and social status put them together as one class. Eventually their roots were cut and they formed different ethnic groups; African Americans and West Indians respectively. Multiple tribal or multi ethnicity migration has become a common phenomenon.

The North American content has always been a land of Immigrants. Even the Native Indians migrated from Asia via Alaska. It is the most accepted theory of the early inhabitants of America over fifty thousand years ago. The land of America was discovered by the Europeans and through their colonization; the rest of the world came to know about it in the fifteenth century. Christopher Columbus landed in the American continent in 1492. His group originally intended to visit India. It was a time in the absence of the manufacturing industry and agricultural and trade was the two main sources of generating wealth. The countries that had abundant natural resources for agriculture engaged in it. Those who do not have much surplus land got involved in trading. It was mostly trade by barter. The Europeans carried guns and wine for trading. The Europeans in many countries had a big problem in preserving meat and other items that can be kept for the cold season. In the absence of the refrigerator, canning and other modern facilities that was brought by the industrial revolution in England, preserving food was a big problem. There was no way of importing fruits, meats and vegetables easily from the tropical zones or from the temperate zones in the southern hemisphere. The thinly populated polar region managed to survive with what they could get in their region.

Spain and Portugal did not do very well in agriculture. They were forced to sail their ships and do business around the world. At that time exporting spices from the Indian sub continent was a very successful business. Those spices were mainly used for preserving meat and other items for the winter season. Though there were spices available in Africa it was not well known to the Europeans. It is the second largest continent in the world. Most parts of Africa were explored only in the 19th century. In the 15th or 16th century, Portugal and Spain came to an unwritten agreement that was more or less an understanding that the world is in a round shape and therefore it will be better if one group moved in the west and the other via the east. They will of course meet in India but in the western part of India by one and other at the eastern side. The Spanish sailed their ship and landed in the new world. Those who landed in the islands of the Caribbean Sea concluded that they got landed in western India on islands and named the region the West Indies. When the team of Columbus met the native people they called the inhabitants of North America "Indians" in an extension of the misapprehension that they landed in India. Even today they are still referred to as Native Indians. The interesting part of it is that that the inhabitants had no idea of India and there was no cultural or any other relationship with them. The Native Indians belonged to hundreds of different tribes, speaking over one thousand languages in which many of them disappeared, their culture, norm of societies, tradition are different. They settled down from the northern polar region to South America. Their languages have not developed a written script and almost all of them had an oral culture only. They were originally hunters and collectors of food. At the early stage they were not confined to one particular area. Later on those wanderers got settled in places and began to do farming. They did have a system of governance for themselves though they had some significant differences. After their colonization they lost their freedom. A systematic elimination took place. Many of them began to learn European languages and left their original languages to die a slow death.

Man is a social animal. He cannot survive by himself. He has the need for directly communicating with fellow human beings, no matter who he is and what type of person he is. Isolation is the worst punishment, it is harder than torture. The two main factors are the natural calamities and that of the man made. In some cases it is the combination these two factors. Let's take the birds in the northern polar region. They could not bear the severe cold during the winter season and made their seasonal migration toward the southern temperate zone and northern part of the tropical zone passing over thousands of kilometers and returned back in this spring. The only difference is that they do not have to obtain visa to enter a territory and there are no restriction or boundaries where other birds claim ownership. The fishes migrate in the oceans at times with the cold and warm ocean currents. We are in an advanced era when man has been trying to migrate to other planets. It is not hard for man to migrate from one location to another taking their history, culture and traditions with them. It is always said that a known devil is better than unknown angel. I do not mean to say that the land that they left is a devil. But the pushing forces might have been the devilish force. In most of the cases of migration there is a deep rooted unpleasant, dissatisfied, sorrowful, victimized, discriminated, segregated, threat to their life and some other negative forces involved in it. The interesting part of this is that people migrate from different countries at various times for many reasons following the same procedure and encounter identical problems. On the other hand the ones who were at the grass root level and the bottom of the society in economic resources would not able to know the ways and means of migrating and not having the resources in moving out. Only the ones who have come to know the ways and having some means are able to migrate successfully.

Historically the pushing forces have played a mayor role in immigration. In historical times when people were in the Stone Age, they were not confined to the nation having a well organized political system. It was a time when most of people were not civilized and enlightened by wisdom. When I mention the word civilization I do not mean to define it in the way President George W Bush frequently did after the attack of September 11, 2001 by terrorists in Washington and New York City.

There are many examples of civilized societies from the ancient world; the Egyptians, The Euphrates, Indus valley, China, the Mohanjodaro, the Lemurian and later on the Greek and Roman and the Mayans of Mexico. The beauty of life of human being is that there are people living in different stages of civilization around the world. We discover that the Stone Age people in the tropical forest in South America around the Amazon River valley, that of the Congo River and in the forests in Philippines There are some primitive societies in the polar regions as well.

Ethnicity and race at times cross their boundaries. There is no separation like the water tide compartments. It overlaps. It gets interpreted differently by many ethnic groups around the world. In South Africa where racial segregation was in existence there was no room for ethnic differences. It was a clear cut racial identity. The while irrespective of British the Dutch, the Germans and all other Europeans and the Jews are placed in one superior basket. The Asians irrespective of their ethnic backgrounds were left in second   place. The third one is the interracial population between the white and non white and the last one was the black, the bulk of the population of having 80% majority. But within each group there were ethnic differences. The blacks had very many ethnic groups within the segregated race. In the modern era the genocide of Adolph Hitler based on the supremacy of the Aryan race and systematic elimination of Jews left a black mark in the history of mankind. On the other hand, the Israelis somehow smuggled Ethiopian Jews. They claim that they are Jews but their way of life is different cultural background is far apart from the Israelis. They are thus considered a different ethnic group.

Some of these classifications are deep rooted in history. Socialists claim to be more of scientific in this theory of human life. They have gone into the economy as the basis of all human behavior. The whole exercise of human activities has been revolving around materialistic interests and that would be the only and final goal of life. It is survival of the fittest.   The identification of nationality, ethnicity, race and all other forms of barriers are meaningless. The concept of free enterprise or capitalism will certainly have two opposite forces. The capitalists will continue in exploiting the labourers. The so called free enterprise system will eventually lead to a monopoly system. The small industries will be swallowed by the big fish. Therefore the majority of the control of resources and the wealth will be in the hands of a few capitalists. It is not necessary for them to look into the well being of the common masses. They do have some concern because they have to market their products and services. The size of the market does not necessarily depend on the size of the population. It depends on the purchasing power. Therefore the system of capitalism would not allow the masses to be too poor.

The Socialists classified the people into two ridge camps; the exploiters and proletariats irrespective of their backgrounds. At the final stage of communism there will be one system of government, one policy and the world will be reach an everlasting system of economic plans. The global concept has taken a different path. According to Marxism all those ethnic, religious, language, colour barriers etc will eventually disappear. Accordingly the worker is a worker. The nature and the interest of the capitalist is only one that is to exploit the labour. In economic terms there are four main factors of production. They are land, labor, capital and entrepreneur. The state monopoly, the government has the overall control and the ownership. The government is formed by the masses. Masses would not go against themselves. Therefore the producers and the consumers are the both sides of the same coin. According to them eventually there will be a common culture in the world. I do not know how far it will go but we cannot wipe out the fact that the concept is still alive in some corners of the globe. Living within the orbit of global values, where to draw the line between preserving their own cultural values while being part of the global family, it should not be a process of assimilation of the minority culture into the majority.

CHAPTER SIXTEEN

STABLE, CONSTANT AND PREDICTABLE CANADIAN FOREIGN POLICY

Barack Obama, 44th President of the United States of America made the announcement of his intention to make Canada the destination of his first presidential visit well before his inauguration. This gesture exhibits his commitment in developing a more cordial relationship with Canada. This nation has been (and still continues to be) a very good ally and has always lent a helping hand in times of need. Therefore we must consider this first state visit an enormous privilege. Mr. Obama with his modified vision from the initial hard-left liberal version met with right wing ideologues and found the way to overcome the current economic recession and strengthen our bilateral relations. This is timely and worthwhile. Canadian doors are wide open to the world and we are very accommodating to the international community in any caliber. The North Pole will never meet the South Pole, but people migrate to Canada from all over the world and their presence has a very high impact in Canadian foreign policy. Eventually, the new immigrants attain Canadian citizenship and their voices are heard in Parliament. Their inclination towards the ancestral homeland somehow influences the parliamentarians in formulating foreign policy.

Canadian performance on the international stage is unique; it clearly shows a country that has been actively involved in many international affairs and has not garnered the world's condemnation nor has it become the target of negative actions. Canada's foreign policy is not merely aimed at ensuring our interests but aims for the best possible outcom. Any dissatisfied reaction meted out to Canada from any other nation is due Canada's support at times, to our good friends south of the border.

The foreign policies of the colonial rulers of the past have an unusually close relationship with their former colonies even though many of them fought bitterly to gain independence and some considered the colonial rulers as exploitative invaders who ruined their ways of life. Their economy was ruined by the introduction of cash crop plantations from the self sufficient economy. Whatever was said and done, the colonial rulers united many small kingdoms and states together under one umbrella which developed into a centralized nation and established a modern way of life. This in turn brought better educational facilities, better transportation and a democratic system of government. The economic investment pre and post independence continues and stabilizes their economy as well. Some of the former colonies claim that their current economic problems are due to colonial rule which nationalized many foreign estates, factories and properties owned and operated by the colonial rulers. Let's take the British Commonwealth nations in which most of the former colonial countries are still active members except for the United State of America which cut off their relationship with Britain. In the Francophone nations, a similar model was developed; likewise Spain, Portugal, Italy, and Germany.

Canada's relationship with Britain and France as a former colony after winning independence in an evolutionary way unlike the revolutionary war of the United States is a very special one and no other country has gained such a privilege. Many countries consider that having such relationship with Canada is a much recognized honour.

The multidimensional Canadian foreign policy of today is a fabric that has been woven on the weft by the hard work, sacrifices and formation of a unique political and cultural identity by the forefathers of this nation. It has been built with the bricks of historical consideration, international humanitarian aid, ideological identity, our impartial stance on the , the bilateral relationship with the U.S.A and keeping Canadian sovereignty intact. By working with the British Commonwealth, La Francophonie, and the North Atlantic Treaty Organization (NATO), the United Nations Organization, the North American Free Trade Agreement (NAFTA), and the European Union, Canadian foreign policy in comparison with other major world players is least concerned about its own self interest. It is multilateral in focus, well balanced and uniform with slight variations irrespective of the ruling party. The foreign policy of many of the worlds' leading nations is very biased and focused more on self interest and is dominated by a few elements. The former colonial powers are more inclined towards their former colonies for example. Although the British foreign policy of today is broader and more diversified having accepted American leadership and by having a better relationship with the former communist countries, the British Commonwealth of 53 countries in four continents have prioritized treatment .

The La Francophonie created in 1968 in Gabon, is similar and also has more emphasis on developing the French language, preserving and promoting heritage values and culture along with economic and political developments. This organization invited the Quebec provincial government, not the Canadian government to join as a sovereign member state. This could be interpreted as a first step towards developing Quebec as an international personality, distinct from that of Canada. We recognize that Quebec was an equal partner at the stage of confederation with the Anglophone provinces. Quebec is also recognized as a distinct society, though not offically and is called a nation within a united Canada, but not a nation by itself. The foreign policy of any nation is based in the federal or central government in a unilateral system. There cannot and should not be two equal organs of government in the same nation in order for our international affairs to be recognized, even though the intentions are not necessarily harmful on either side. This is a very serious matter and must serve as a reminder to us that there cannot be two voices from the same country on international issues, though there certainly can be diverse opinions. If the invitation would have gone through the federal government to Quebec with its consent it would have been much appreciated. It is true that Canada was a British colony while New France was a French colony later captured by the British Empire. After the former French colony was amalgamated, it became a member of the British Commonwealth. Canada as a whole has never been under French rule so it is hard to be considered a member of La Francophonie, but we also have to consider the interest of Quebec in its meaningful affiliation with this organization. Now the problem is that by passing over the federal government in a way in which it is not given due recognition is very painful, if not an insult. The recent celebration of the 400th anniversary of the establishment of Quebec City in which the presence of Queen Elizabeth II as the Queen of Canada was considered, though she did not attend, is one recent example. Canada has an exceptional relationship with both the United Kingdom and France and so the issue of inviting Queen Elizabeth II to the celebration raised passions on both sides.

Canadian foreign policies at the early stage were obliged to follow the same path as the British Empire and it was designed and executed by the Empire. The counterpart in America, the thirteen colonies, won their independence and formed their own foreign polices. It was time when the world was not closely connected and international affairs except for colonial matters did not dominate. Before the confederation was formed, Canada did not have any independent voice and had to dance to the tune of the British pipers, though according to many this was done willingly. During the intercontinental disputes such as Nootka Convention war of 1812, the Rush-Bagot Treaty, the Webster-Ashburton Treaty and Oregon treaty of 1854, all of those disputes were settled by the British. Even after the confederation was formed, the British Empire expected Canada to help Britain when they were in need by making use of the fact that the Queen of Canada was also the Monarch of Britain. When Britain had a battle in Sudan in 1884-85 Canada was expected to send supports to join the British troops but Canada was reluctant to join. But the Governor General privately raised 386 voyageurs at the expense of Britain.

Canada participated in the First World War because Canada was still viewed as a British subject and loyal to the Monarchy. Our participation in Vimy Ridge helped Canada establish itself as a force to be reckoned with. The Second World War was a different matter. Canada did not get involved initially; however after the attack on Pearl Harbour both Canada and the United States joined the allies. Canada's involvement was viewed as a moral obligation; everyone was helping in the war effort and if anyone tried to opt out, this was viewed with scorn. However, there are many examples of our refusal as a nation to get involved in international conflicts. When former president Nasser nationalized the Suez Canal, Britain went to war with Egypt and a request was made to Canada to support Britain with direct involvement. Canada declined and Britain was not at all pleased. When American coalition forces began the war against terrorism in Iraq and Afghanistan, Canada's former prime Minster John Chrétien refused to join because it was not sanctioned by the United Nations. But Tony Blair the British Prime Minster supported and joined the coalition forces. So in spite of Canada's close relationship with America rather than Britain, Canada kept itself away from involvement in the war in the early stage.

Trade, investment, immigration, political ideas, media and literature in Canada is strongly influenced by the United States of America. Canadian ties with America have become very close and our way of life mirrors that of America. Over 80 % of Canadian exports go to America and until very recently, Canada was the largest exporter to the States until China claimed up and pushed Canada to second place. Canada being very dependable and influential in many ways has raised some fears that Canada may become the 51st undeclared state. There is reasonable fear among some Canadians that the high level of influence in many areas including economic dependency, may lead to the control of political, economical, and military power of Canada by the U.S and this will become a challenge to the sovereignty of Canada as it used to be by Britain. It would not be that easy to draw a demarcation line between the two.

America is the only super power in the world that has a 13 trillion dollar economy and the highest level of influence in the world. Canada cannot easily deviate from America and become a close ally with any other powers. Canada's only bordering state is America and the reality is that we have to be tolerant and flexible when dealing with this neighbour. I know this sounds as though Canada is not a sovereign state, but it still important that we respect the power of our neighbor to the south.

American foreign policy is very complex and has multiple agendas. Mr. George W. Bush in his final speech on January 15, 2009 at the White House said" We've made our alliances stronger, we've made our nation safer and we have made the world freer". America has interfered in many foreign countries internal affairs at times to serve the best interest of this super power. America has at times unpredictably crossed over to support the enemy of a nation to whom support was provided. It happened during the era. America supported Ethiopia in the war between Eritrea and Ethiopia during the regime of Emperor Haile Sellasie and when Menguestu Hailre Mariam dethroned the emperor and sided with the Soviet Union, both the super powers crossed over. As someone said about Britain during the colonial era "Britain has no permanent friends or permanent enemies but permanent interest". This sentiment can also be applied to the United States both historically and in recent times. For example Saddam Hussein and Osama Bin Laden were good friends and unfortunately turned against America and America had to take alternative steps. America has to protect the rights of Israelis to survive in the Middle East and compromise with the Arab nations. America also has to protect itself from anticipated attacks by the Russians and established anti-missile defense deals with Poland and the Czech Republic. America made a free trade agreement with China without much consideration towards Canada's long time trade relationship. American isolationist foreign policy was given up to a larger extent and Mr. George W. Bush the former American President attended the 2008 Olympic Games in China and there are signals that their might be some changes to the disconnected stance of American foreign policy. The former Spanish colonies in South America gained independence in the early 1800s and America declared its opposition to European interference in the Americas, but today they are closely associated with the USA.

At the international level, Canada has taken positions and acted in ways that have not made the United States very pleased. Canada established its diplomatic relationship with the People's Republic of China on 13th October 1970; the USA became established on 1st of January 1979.

Canadian foreign policy had been influenced by the between the period of 1945 and 1991. Although Canada was a middle level developed nation and was not intending to blindly support any super power, this move proved to be beneficial. Although the Soviet Union formed a socialist system of rule in 1917, it reached the super power level after the Second World War in 1945. It is crystal clear that the core of the was not a rivalry between two empires but more of an ideological war between the centralized economy in a one party system of government based on socialist philosophy and the decentralized free enterprise system of economy in a democratic system of government. According to the Socialists, their system of government is a democratic government in the form of proletariat dictatorship. Canada being a state based on compassionate social policies and democratic government could not be part of the Soviet Block. Canada in terms of its ideology agreed to disagree in order to be in line with the Soviet Block and Canada never isolated the Soviet Union or refused to cooperate with them in many other international issues. It does not mean that Canada was under the umbrella of the American block. Canada had been practicing under a similar system of government and had a common economic system in operation. Certainly on the grounds of common interest, the inclination of Canada towards America was in a different context. The former Soviet Block threatened America and some of their associates and certain measures were taken to discredit the socialist system. By exposing things such as the deprivation of fundamental human rights including freedom of expression, this encouraged citizens of the Eastern Block to migrate to non-Communist states such as Canada and they were accepted as refugees. During and for a period after the Canada's foreign policy remained as it was without many fundamental changes, not unlike the cold Canadian winter.

Canada's relationship with many international countries regarding the migration of new comers has made a very unique impact. Canada accepts more refugees and immigrants per capita than most nations in the world and the recent immigration policy is unbiased and more accommodative in nature. The indirect measures of limiting immigrants to Canada other than Europe were eliminated by the Immigration Act made in the early and middle parts of the last century. There are many immigrants who have migrated from Eastern Europe, countries in Africa, Asia, Latin America and Australia, who have made their new settlements and are now leading a wonderful life in a strange land. It is not only the implementation of foreign policy, but also the effect of Canadian multiculturalism.

The Canadian government generally discourages any form of war and advocates and tries its best in preventing the eruption of any war or armed conflict. The formation of this nation itself was based on the negotiated transfer of power from Britain. Canada settled territorial and boundary disputes with mutual agreements. When a conflict arose on boundary disputes between the USA and Canada in 1984 when the court of International Justice ruled on the maritime boundary in the Gulf of Marine, Canada accepted the verdict. In a similar dispute cropped up with France on the maritime boundary surrounding the Islands of St. Pierre and Miquelon, Canada accepted the International Court of Arbitration ruling. Once its goes beyond its influence, Canada prefers to keep itself away from direct involvement in war except if it is absolutely necessary like World War One and Two and a few others. Canada does not fuel armed conflicts and war by trying to sell arms through the back door or front door.

There are unresolved disputes in northern Canada with the USA and other nations. Canadian sovereignty over the North West passage representing territorial waters has been challenged by the USA as it is part of international waters. The American reinforced oil tanker the Manhattan sailed through the North West passage in 1969 followed by the icebreaker Polar Sea in 1985 without getting permission from Canada because they claimed that it was in international waters. America was adamant in rejecting Canada's claims that it was the internal waters of Canada and they wanted to have the absolute freedom of navigation. At last a compromise was reached in 1988 by an agreement on Artic cooperation. America would have the consent of Canada in navigating in the said body of water. In 2006 David Wilkins the American Ambassador to Canada opposed Mr. Steven Harper's proposed plan to deploy military icebreakers in the Artic to detect interlopers and assert Canadian sovereignty over those waters. The final settlement has not been reached, but Canada is still waiting for a peaceful settlement after negotiations.

Protective measures against international terrorism are the latest concern in terms of the international policy of Canada. Canada is not an exception on the target list of terrorist groups and Canada cannot handle this alone. It is a cyclone that has destroyed some nations and continues to expand to others. Canadian support and participation in some of the measures initiated south of the border in collaboration with highly targeted and other supportive nations is unavoidable and Canada has to face the consequences. Both the political parties who have been ruling this country alternatively or otherwise agreed upon this. It is much worse than the and penetrates into the internal affairs and takes destructive actions against the innocent civilian population. The threat posed by militants and international operations of terrorist organizations have a network all around the world and the central body coordinates its activities and runs its operations.

Canada is extremely careful in handling such issues. I praise the Canadian government in how it handled the September 11, 2001 attacks in the US by keeping the peace and urging calm. In spite of all that has been happening, Canadians have acted very rationally. As a country and as a society we drew the line with the terrorists and the rest of the law abiding Canadian citizens who practice the same religious faith. Of course in any society there might be some emotional reactions, but the government of Canada and the rest of Canadians ignored those remote incidents and continued to extend their hands in making peace and harmony. The tolerance, generosity and kindness shown by Canada should not be considered a weakness. But the threat and danger from terrorists continues to exist in a more sophisticated way. The reaction to any destructive action on Canadian soil may certainly pave the way to changes in Canadian foreign policy and it is hoped that this will not happen.

Canadian foreign policy is very generous and even considers international affairs that do not directly have any effect. Our foreign policy investigates international matters in terms of the way it should be handled, not what is in it for us. Built-in Canadian interest in international policy is a very small element compared with many other nations. It makes Canada a unique player on the international field.

CHAPTER SEVENTEEN

UPPER CANADA BECOMES SUPER CANADA

(The Potential and Prosperity of Ontario)

When I first arrived in Toronto from Montreal after a short stay of three months on the first of January 1987, the amazing attraction was not the CN tower but a quote on the vehicle license plate '*Yours to discover*'. A long time ago, Christopher Columbus discovered America mainly in the eyes of the western world, but we Ontarians could not discover the nature of the people from the natives to newcomers and from physical features to climate control. I consider Ontario as my first primer in the national and international curriculum in my process of life long learning and I am fortunate to be a privileged student.

Though the name Ontario is derived from the Iroquoian phrase meaning 'beautiful lake' and though it was applied to Lake Ontario the term eventually included its surrounding area. Later on, historians suggest that Ontario might have come from another native word 'Entouhonorous' meaning 'the people'. The territory was renamed Upper Canada in 1791 to relate to the upper course of the St. Lawrence River and when Quebec and Ontario were amalgamated it was renamed as "west Canada". In 1841 we returned to square one with the original name of Ontario.

The extensive diversity and complexity of the physical features and the human resources of Ontario is an asset and it gives an additional strength that keeps the province sound and solid in all aspects of the lives of the people from the pre-historic era to the modern world in the 21st century.

Ontario, the second largest province of 1,076,395 sq km in size in Canada, will continue to be prosperous in its economy due to various favorable factors including the physical features of the land. Most of the rocks in Ontario are 600 million years old and are a solid pre Cambrian rock. Based on the physical features, Ontario can be classified into three main regions; the flat land around the Hudson Bay region, the Canadian Shield in the middle of the province covered with forest and the lowlands surrounded by the fertile St. Lawrence River. Once it was said by someone in the middle of the ocean "Water, water, everywhere but not a drop of water to drink". In Ontario, abundant fresh water is everywhere in the form of lakes and numerous rivers and in the north in a solid form as ice. Canada shares with the United States four out of five of the Great Lakes and these lakes are the world's biggest bodies of fresh water. Apart from the rich fertile soil in some regions there are areas where it is not suitable for arable farming but the sub soils are abundant in valuable minerals such as copper and nickel. This is the particular case with Sudbury which has the world's largest deposits of nickel ore at the Ontario shore of Lake Superior. Gold mines are located at Porcupine Lake and Kirkland Lake and the first oil wells in North America were sunk on the Ontario peninsula and other minerals such silver were discovered and this has also enriched Ontario.

Ontario is also rich in vegetation and varieties of animals All around the province, numerous types of animals and birds can be found such as deer, coyotes, caribou, wolves, foxes, polar bears, raccoons, mink, weasels, and wolverines, horses, cattle and other livestock, muskrats, lemmings, beaver, squirrels, chipmunks and domestic animals crown the beauty of our province and provide a source of income from dairy farming, the meat industry, hides and furs and the tourism industry. The water bodies also have different types of species, such as herons, ducks, sandpipers, fish, carp, white perch, trout, Chinook salmon and wonderful birds that seasonally migrate from the north in the winter season. Ontario is very rich with forests that generate both local and export income as well.

The existence of human beings in Ontario began long before the historic era. The first wave of migration came from Asia via the Bering Strait land bridge almost thirty thousand years ago and arrived in Ontario through the west. The First Nations did not belong to a single ethnicity. Their customs, dialogue, traditions and religious practices varied from one another but there are some similarities. Some of their customs and beliefs and habits are similar to those of certain Africans. I would cite an example based on my experience of living in Africa, of the custom of the burial of privileged personalities in the First Nations culture. It is very elaborate with the belief that the souls will survive in another form and the burial of the deceased favorite things and supporting persons is another commonality. When it comes to the upbringing of children there are many differences that have been noticed. Some of the Ontario First Nations people gave much freedom to the children and they believed in the self reliance of children rather than obedience and kids were not punished or scolded. Their belief in the spiritual well being of all living things such as plants and animals was not based on the belief that man is superior, rather on stewardship. Their beliefs actually have some parallels with Hinduism. According to Hindu theology, all living things have similar souls and they are interrelated and man is a product of the evolutionary karmic process.

The second wave of migration came from Europe in the sixteenth century and the settlement began from the east coast towards the west. They intended to visit India and purchase spices and gold and by accident landed on the North American shores. But the Portuguese discovered fish in the Canadian waters and were quite pleased and this wiped out their disappointment. Later on they came with the purpose of trading. Fur bearing animals such as beavers were the center of attraction and in the absence of money, exchanging knives, guns, and whisky was very popular though it was uncommon. The trading was very much liked by the native chiefs and it was easy for the European traders to make a profit. Beavers were easy to hunt and it were very abundant in Ontario and Quebec and it became at the initial stage, the main trade article and the resources of a wide range of animals brought many Europeans to this province. The traditional way of trading between the natives improved more in terms of quantity and the exchange of new goods pleased many native chiefs. The challenges and fear around the ownership of land and their right to rule themselves was a concern. In 1670 though the British claimed a monopoly on the fur trade, the French exported a portion of the fur to France and the British King Charles II was not pleased with this. It was the period of time that the French Catholic missionaries established their missions in Ontario and converted some natives to Christianity. The men converted a little more easily, not the women because they were very powerful in their families and held on to their religion. Their society granted more freedom to women more than the French in their society. The missionaries antagonized the natives by condemning their religions as demonic and of the Devil. It was very hard and dangerous and some of the missionaries learnt their languages and picked up similar views and slowly converted them. The Jesuits were busy in spreading their religious message extensively among the Huron. It was the time the French in Quebec got into politics and pitted one side against the other by siding with the Huron and Algonquians against a powerful tribe of Iroquois leading to terrible results. The Iroquois got angry and began to take revenge and declared a war in July 1648 and raided the mission in Huronia. On 15th March 1649 the Iroquois over ran two more missions and captured, tortured and killed a few of the Jesuits. Their aim was also to control the flourishing fur trade and it turned into a fight for controlling the trade in beaver. The Beaver war continued for years and many natives who fought with bow and arrow were easily killed with guns by the Europeans. The French outnumbered the British and had better control and they operated their fur trade from Montreal and got involved in Ontario as well. They were the ones who explored the complexity of the network of the water links between the rivers along with the great Lakes. Charles II, the King of England took a very brave initiative in penetrating into Ontario and building up influences. The Hudson's Bay Company was well established and competed with the French fur traders.

The demographic pattern of Ontario compared with Quebec was sparsely populated by the Europeans. The America revolution between the years of 1775-1781 pushed the British loyalists to flee to the North and a sizeable number in thousands came to Ontario and settled down.

The British government realized that in order to utilize the abundant natural resources and enrich the land they not only had to encourage trading but also have permanent settlements that practiced agriculture. New immigrants of course in this case British immigrants were granted land at the token price of six pence per acre and a very small related cost. Later on, immigrants from non British and French origins were migrating to Canada. For example, the German migration began as early as 1750. The improvement in the European economy and the rapid increase in population were the pushing factor and the rich soil and supply of water was the pulling factors that encouraged new immigrants to migrate and settle down and clear the forest and begin farming.

The strength of the British in many ways reached that of the French and brought some silent confrontations between the French Quebecers and the British descendants and the British parliament passed the Constitutional Act of 1791. This Act split the colony around the St Lawrence River and the Great Lakes into Upper Canada -Ontario and Lower Canada- Quebec.

The influx of many American civilians and their growing influence alarmed the Ontarians and as they predicted, the American military invasion turned into a war declared by the Americans on Britain on 18th June 1812. The war was blessing in disguise because the British settlers, the French settlers and the natives kept their differences aside and united   under one umbrella and fought against the American invaders. The Quebecers did not want to be a part of the United States for fear that it would crush French identity and put it in the melting pot.   One of the prime causes for the war that was initiated by the Americans was the attraction of the St. Lawrence River as a strategic gateway. This river is the backbone of both Quebec and Ontario and under any aggression or pressure it cannot be compromised by anyone. I am pretty sure that the navigation on the river will be better facilitated in the future. The volume of water and navigation are vital to both the provinces. At the initial stage, the Americans had an upper hand in the war but at the end they were defeated and the war ended on 24 December 1814. The American claimed success in this war reminded me of the Vietnam War. At one point in time, the Americans wanted to get out of the war after losing over fifty thousand of its soldiers and war related participants and declared that they came to peace with honour.

The war brought both the French settlers and the British settlers closer to a common cause and a mutual understanding was developed. Based on this turning point it was decided that it would be better to join both the provinces Upper and Lower Canada and have a solidified region as a single province. By recognizing their unique identities, they named Ontario as West Canada and Quebec as East Canada in 1841. However, many conflicts, contradictions, and disagreements arose and this brought on an unpleasant political tone. An example of this is that the location of the Capital was not unanimously accepted and it was shifted from Kingston to Montréal and finally moved to Ottawa, the city located at the border of both provinces. Even today, certain federal government offices are located on the Québec side and the rest are in Ontario. Finally, the British Empire gave birth to the new nation of Canada on 1st July 1867 with the provinces of Ontario, Québec, New Brunswick and Nova Scotia.

During the period between the declaration of confederation and the beginning of the depression of 1929-1932, Ontario modernized and industrialized very fast and modern tools began to replace hand made traditional tools. Large scale agricultural activities brought a better standard of living and expansion of Canadian communication with other provinces made Ontario the centre of economic activities and brought more employment and wealth. Ontario contributed to half of Canada's industrial production. Ontario's manufacturing industry was mainly concentrated in a belt that ran from Oshawa passing through Toronto, Mississauga and Hamilton, all the way up to the south shore of Lake Simcoe. At that time, Ontario had almost half of the Canadian population and people's lives became easier and more comfortable. Although tremendous progress and prosperity uplifted Ontario, the economic recession of 1870 in the Atlantic Provinces adversely affected the Ontario economy and a decline in exports of agricultural products. The rapid expansion of the manufacturing industries and factory establishment brought better working conditions and safety measures

The rural population began to migrate to urban areas to find manufacturing jobs instead of farming and working in primary industries and a sharp decline in the rural population resulted. Significant rural areas were modernized and converted into urban cities and towns. At times when people could not find jobs in the urban cities they returned back to their villages.

The economic depression of 1929 lasted for almost four years and resulted in a slow down in production and a breakdown in some financial institutions. Bankruptcy closed down some factories permanently, some jobs permanently disappeared and the high rate of unemployment in the construction sector and service industries put the unemployment rate at 20%. The unemployment rate among the male population was greater than the female population because the wages women were paid was lower. The economy suffered very badly on the basis of a single industry like Oshawa and Windsor which mainly depended on the automobile industry. The relief program for unemployed workers drained the resources of the provincial and federal government. Once there is an economic recession or depression prejudice towards new immigrants and a kind of racial tension can arise.

Coupled with economic depression, World War II brought another disaster to Ontario and it brought personal tragedies, destruction, loss of solders, and sluggish economic uncertainty. Ontarians supported the involvement of Canada in the First World War due to backing up Britain and in the Second World War, their support was against Germany.

The government of Ontario and the federal government realized how the common people suffered in the world wars and the economic depression. The government wanted to give more assistance and expanded the area of social services to compensate and assist the veterans in living a balanced life. Activities on reconstruction, resettlement and readjustment   dominated in the post war period. The baby boom brought more production of baby products and in due course, the expansion of the nursery, elementary, secondary, college and other post secondary institutions received more grants for both capital and operational expenditures.

The current system of education in Ontario unfailingly catered to the students and comparatively, universal compulsory education services have almost met their targets. But among the First Nations it has yet to penetrate deeply. Our system of education has to be more concerned around meeting the challenges of technology, life, and educational changes. The drop out rate is pretty high and 29% do not complete their school education and their future lives have to pass through a draft sea. Since the decline of the natural birth rate the government can spend more to develop a higher quality educational experience. Most of the advanced educational institutions are concentrated in a triangle belt in the south and the northerners do not have access to that kind of program. The expansion of the mode of electronic facilities for them is another pressing need.

State sponsored medical services without any service charges provided to the public through OHIP consumes almost 40% of the revenue and still in Ontario over a million Ontarians do not have family doctors. The establishment of an electronic filing system in this modern world would provide easy access at any time to ones medical history. This system would prove to be very useful, especially in the case of accidents or if the patient is in a coma and cannot give necessary medical details. At one point I would say our health care system itself is sick and it needs if not surgery, immediate treatment.

The baby boomers are becoming seniors and their medical expenses are rapidly increasing and it is our obligation to provide them with required medical services. Other dependants are our children although the decline in birth rate is somewhat reduced, the traditional expenses for rearing children are increasing. These days in most families both the parents have to work to meet the expenses of the high standard of living and it is no more depending solely on a single bread winner. The daycare facilities are inadequate and costly. This issue has been addressed by many groups but somehow the increase in funding and investments allocated for it do not resolve the problem that is faced by low income earners. Thanks to the federal government for providing the universal child care payment for the lower income earners.

The rapid increase in the cost of living in the urban cities and towns do not go parallel to the rate of minimum wages and many Ontarians cannot manage with their full time earnings and wind up working in a part time job to supplement their income. This results in having inadequate time with the family and family values are deteriorating.

The increase in the crime rate is a big challenge. Innocent citizens who have been leading a law abiding life and have never gotten involved in any kind of dispute are scared to move freely, some of them are even confined at home alone. The rates of robbery, rape, vandalism, and gun violence are increasing and the men in uniform face a high risk in discharging their day to day duties. When it comes to the children, action movies and video games are motivating and encouraging the children to participate in violence. Of course compare our cities of the same caliber and size with other cities around the world, ours are more peaceful and have low crime rate. We do not want to compare with other cities; we prefer to compare with our past.

One of the contributing factors for the increasing crime rate is the inadequate instillation of moral values in our educational system. I do understand that having religious aspects on the school curriculum will certainly disrupt the social harmony in a multi cultural society having many faiths if the lessons go beyond the basics. But we should also understand that in the past, the religious institutions played a major role in the administration of towns and cities and village councils but today there is no place for them other than participating at ceremonial functions. There was a well established pattern of life and the social norms regulated the life of individuals in a community, it played a wonderful role and its command was unwritten laws. Modern society does not give much room for it and at times the human rights code has been interpreted conveniently. Maintaining a high level of family values establishes a social harmony and an improved family life.

Most of our activities have been influenced and geared to the economy. The strength and the weakness and ups and downs have an impact on various sectors of life. Ontario has a very strong and diversified economic structure and does not depend solely on the yield of a single commodity but the growth rate compared with the rest of the provinces is on the downside. Ontario, one of the leading "have" provinces should not lean towards the "have not" side. The entrepreneurs require more incentives and protection; the workers want their pay increased and need better job protection. Foreign investors have to be lobbied and encouraged to come and invest more in our province. The American protectionist methods and other export restrictions made by the American government have to be negotiated and North American free trade has to be maintained. If not, then why not develop a Canada-America free trade agreement and eliminate import duties and other restrictions between the two countries. Encourage American tourists to visit and spend their holidays in a wonderful country. We have to make a greater effort to welcome movie producers from Hollywood to come and shoot films here. To some extent, the elimination of inter provincial barriers in trade also have to be reviewed. We should not put all of the export eggs in a big basket and some in a plastic bag; rather we must focus on diversifying with new trade partners and redirect a part of our exports to other countries. It is not an easy task but not impossible if we take a strong leadership position.

The lack of skilled man power and the limited supply from local sources are pressuring us to have more immigrants. So far over fifty percent of the arrivals to Canada migrate to Ontario but the allocation per capita for settlement programs such as LINC (Language Instruction for Newcomers to Canada) and other settlement programs to Ontario is lower than in other provinces. Ontario is on the verge of utilizing the right to have the province select new immigrants like some of Western provinces and Quebec and it has to be more considerate. We must also discourage the brain drain from Ontario. For example, there is a shortage of doctors in this province whereas some of the doctors and qualified nurses are moving down south for better pay and other facilities. The internal migration from the other provinces recently has been partially deviated to oil rich Alberta and

Saskatchewan and that has made the dependency of relying on new immigrants even greater.

Historically speaking, this essay would be incomplete without mentioning Alexander Graham Bell who invented the telephone and brought glory to our great nation. A Scottish born Bell grew up near Brantford, Ontario and worked as a speech therapist and conceived the idea for his invention at the age of 27. It was on 3rd of August 1876 in the Dominion Telegraph office in Mount Pleasant that his creation was unveiled with a few lines from William Shakespeare. Who would have thought that his invention would one day revolutionize communication to the point where we have phones that can fit inside our pocket?

Upper Canada should always remain up in Canada and it is the hard work, vision, commitment and awareness of every Ontarian that will keep its name up always.

CHAPTER EIGHTEEN

TORONTO- THE MODEL RAINBOW CITY DIVERSITY OUR STRENGTH

It was a pleasant afternoon in the beginning of the year 1998. Torontonians were in a celebratory mood regarding the amalgamation of the six municipalities of Scarborough, York, North York, Toronto and Etobicoke into one wonderful entity we like to call the mega city. The invites for the celebration were heading towards the city hall with pride and enthusiasm and I was among them. The long awaited historic swearing in ceremony began with cheers and I noticed that Mr. Mel Lastman, the first mayor elect, was well dressed and wore the Jewish kippah (skull cap) on his head. This affirmed his identity and exhibited the Jewish belief that he is not on the top of the world and that the almighty god is and presides over all. With this symbolism in mind, we participated in the swearing in ceremony with much enthusiasm. This elevated my morale and impression of Torontonians and how they have broad, accommodative and embracing minds. I could not help but notice many invitees who came from all corners of the world happily participating in this ceremony. My mind went back to a time, not very long ago in Toronto, where in some of the remote restaurants notices were placed on the doors stating that *"Dogs and Jews are not allowed"*. Times have changed. Long before this ceremony, during Mr. Lastman's election campaign all of the supporters, volunteers and assistants were all members of various multi-ethnic groups and almost all ethnicities were well represented. Toronto the city of multicultural rainbows. This diverse and complex city exhibits the peaceful coexistence of Torontonians with new comers who come from over 170 countries from the six continents, who belong to over hundred ethnicities and speak over one hundred and sixty languages and practice many faiths certainly elevate Toronto's status as a model city in this modern world.

The recent rapid growth of this city in terms of demographic patterns, economic expansion, extended national and provincial administrative organs and having a bulk of skilled workers in the service industries along with improved infrastructure has placed Toronto as the largest city in Canada with over 2.5 million residents. Toronto is also the fifth most populous municipality in North America. It is also one of the top financial centers in the world and is the economic capital of Canada along with its recognition as a global city. Compared with other large cities such as London England, New York in the USA, Paris France, Tokyo Japan, and Bombay India, Toronto has well balanced growth in all aspects and does not lack or have deficiencies in certain areas of urbanization. I would cite a couple of examples to illustrate this point. In many cities, certain areas are recognized as the residential areas for the cream of the crop. These areas are of such a high caliber and poor people can not even dream about living in these rather exclusive areas. In contrast, there are areas where the bulk of the population lives in poverty. Hunger, anger, violence, along with frustration, in these very densely populated areas with inadequate social amenities is a way of life. It is not unusual for entire families with parents and grown children to live in one room with no privacy for adults, no room for doing school work and certainly no where for the children to play. It is also very common in these urban slums to have no access to clean running water. I happened to meet one such laborer in one of these cities who had only two sets of clothes. He was wearing one of them and the second pair was in laundry for washing. Once I met him at the laundry where he paid for the services and received the washed clothes. He then moved into a corner of the laundry room and changed into the clean clothes. He spent his only weekend off by purchasing a drink at a corner store that was made from rotten fruit and some insects and became very intoxicated. Many of these people are forced by the ignorance of the government or the so called absolute liberty in free enterprise where everyone has the key to open the door to accumulate wealth and climb up the economic ladder. Certainly such a poor labour class exists in many cities around the world, but not in Toronto. Those circumstances push them into indulging in many unlawful activities and I spent some time with them and they expressed their belief that their life is destined to suffer and the successful and rich people are cheats, liars and steal public money. Those areas are mostly centers of crimes such as drug trafficking, prostitution, murder for money, theft and so on. I do not mean to say that these things do not happen in Toronto but the amount is very limited and confined to small pockets here and there. I understand the residences of lower income earners have a lot of problems and inadequate facilities but compared with the cities I have just mentioned the gravity of those problems is minimal.

Any stranger who visits Toronto can easily notice the underground railway, basement apartments, and the underground shopping complexes in the downtown but they would not be able to hear about the underground economic activities in operation. In some cities the amount of wealth in the underground economy and income generated exerts great control not only in the economy but also political power. In some cities, the politicians or the rulers cannot be in operation without their blessing and anyone who tries to oppress or eliminate them will simply "disappear". Although the size of the underground economy cannot be fully measured or exposed, we can arrive at a conclusion which is close to the reality of the situation. As far as I know, such a strong underground economy is not a threat to Toronto.

Toronto is one of the most well planned, structured and maintained cities in the world. The magnificent growth of the city began naturally with limited planning because the size of the population was low and a low number of new immigrants migrated to the city. In the absence of big factories, there was no need to have a concentration of workers settlements around the factory and settlement in the city was brought into the planning of the municipalities. I am very certain that in those days they might not have dreamed of today's growth. Since the 1960's the growth rate has been unbelievable and the municipal government of Toronto, with the help of the provincial government planned the further physical development well and Toronto expanded to the hinterlands. Toronto is among the very few, if not the only city that has wide open space with untouched virgin land. The planning thus became unavoidable and all modern physical structures had to be approved before the construction work began.

I had a very wonderful experience in Toronto a few days after I arrived from Montreal in early 1987. I did not own a car, and being a new immigrant, had to apply for a driver's license. My mode of transportation was commuting and this gave me a chance to write articles and read books. As usual I left my home in Scarborough, got into the rapid transportation, reached Kennedy station and got into the subway train. It was heading towards Kipling station. When the trained passed three or four stops the door of the compartment where I was seated had some mechanical problems and could not be opened. The train was in motion and after passing three stations, two mechanics came in, put up a sign saying that the subway door was under repair and started their work. When the train reached Sherburne station everything had been brought back to normal and the passengers who entered the train at that station had no idea of what went wrong and how it was repaired. The effective operation and efficiency of those technicians impressed me a lot and got deep down into my heart. It is one of a handful of unforgettable experiences that I will never forget for all my life. It was amazing and exhibits the efficiency of the operation of other institutions and I neither cite it as a typical example nor an exceptional incident, but it could be generalized about the effective operation of government and non government institutions

In spite of the increasing number of crimes compared with the past, Toronto has been and still is one of the safest cities in the world and this trend of increasing crime is global and not peculiar to Toronto. Toronto has one of the lowest homicide rates and cities such Atlanta, Boston, Washington, and New York City in the United States and Vancouver Canada has higher rates of crime than Toronto and this is enviable. While writing this article, the right honorable Prime Minister was in the city of Vancouver after a chain of homicides and the Justice Minster introduced tougher measures against such crimes and said that eventually more light would be shed on such cases. The rates of theft and robbery are also a concern and Toronto is ranked in a much better position. The effectiveness of the Canadian positive approach has made an excellent impact on new immigrants, in certain cases two or more ethnic groups fought against each other and had a mountain full of hatred in their country of origin. But after getting used to the Canadian way of living they began to intermingle and realized that it was not the entire population from the opposed community that was the cause of their suffering but certain forces.

Toronto, the biggest, most populous city in Canada is the center of catering to a large number of new immigrants. The increasing trend of new immigrants bringing their heritage values and preserving them while embracing Canadian values is widely respected and honoured in this city. The reflection of the cosmopolitan and international multi ethnic nature makes Toronto one of the world's most diverse cities. In terms of the percentage of non- native and early European settlers; the number of foreign born Canadians accounted for around 20% but its percentage in Toronto is a little less than a half (49%) of the population

The city of Toronto was officially incorporated and named on 6th March 1834 by Mayor Lyon Mackenzie and its 175th anniversary is a grand and historical event. It was renamed by Lt. Governor John Graves Simcoe in 1793 as York and elevated to the capital of Upper Canada. Later on to avoid confusion with the city of New York in the United States of America and for various other reasons, York was renamed as Toronto. The origin of the name differs. According to the Seneca word "giyando" it refers to a village called Taiaiagon. According to Mohawks the word it is "tkaronto' meaning there are trees standing in the water around Humber River around the northern end of Lake Simcoe. Most likely it derived from the Iroquois word 'rkaronto". As any Torontonian will tell you, there are many nicknames for Toronto such as the big smoke, the Queen City, and Hogtown

Pre historically the native people mainly the Huron and Iroquois who arrived in Canada via the west settled down in Toronto and around the great lakes and adjoining river areas. The forest area was very helpful for hunting and the abundant source of fresh water for agriculture was a blessing for them to settle down conveniently. Since the sixteenth century the European settlers arrived mainly from Britain and France. The French traders founded Fort Rouille in downtown Toronto in 1750 but this was short lived. During the American Revolution there was an unexpected influx of British settlers who were United Empire Loyalists. When the immigration gates were widely opened from time to time many immigrants migrated to Toronto for many reasons which included; easy access for employment in a variety of areas, Toronto was a safe city for living in peace and harmony, better transportation facilities, and a cordial socio-economic atmosphere. These are some of the exact same reasons that many people choose to make Toronto their home even today.

Its growth from a triangular shaped city with only four blocks running from the current Parliament Street in the east to Front Street in the south and Richmond Street in the north and York Street in the west gradually expanded in all directions. The European settlers who came from the east contributed to the development of Toronto. Their hard work, new technology, determination, and enthusiasm made the reputation of Toronto taller than the CN tower.

Originally the capital of this region was situated at Newark at Niagara-on the lake and shifted to Toronto. The role of the great lake was much more than the supplying of fresh water; it was the most convenient access point for navigation which was the popular mode of transportation within the continent to foreign counties particularly to Europe. The St. Lawrence River, the gate way of Canada with few interruptions gave a way for Europeans to penetrate into the interior lands and set up successful trade establishments and local businesses. In the absence of an extensive network of land transportation and of course, air transportation, navigation was the only commonly available mode of transportation and this was one of the determining factors to locate the capital close to the lake. The city of Newark was attached to three out of the five great lakes.

The first municipal election for Toronto was held on 27th March 1834, twenty one days after Toronto was incorporated as a city on 6th March 1834. The election was called by the Lt. Governor. Sir John

Colborne and most of the elections were held in taverns where people commonly met. It was an entirely new exercise and all elected councilors had no clue as to their responsibilities and limitations of rights and procedures. All councilors were brand new and started learning from scratch and built up a system of governing and cited an example to other municipalities in most of the functional aspects.

It was in 1834 and onward that the massive construction of buildings, bridges and roads began and continued. People were very busy in deforesting the land densely populated with hard wood and soft wood virgin forests. The number of streets grew to 85 streets in 1840. The present generation and the new immigrants may find it hard to imagine overall life in Toronto in the absence of modern roads, vehicles, and pipe born water. There was an improperly built in harbour and navigation was the main source of long distance transportation. The city had only one newspaper called the "Upper Canada Gazette" with a very limited circulation. It was a different scene back then, but compared with the surrounding areas, Toronto was an advanced city.

In 1841 when Upper Canada and Lower Canada were amalgamated, Upper Canada was named 'Ontario' and Lower Canada was named 'Quebec", Toronto ceased to be the capital.

The growth of Toronto gradually extended to the hinterlands and the interdependency between the two brought fruits for both of them. In the GTA, there are twenty five municipalities and the inter link and interdependency benefits both sides, and the so called 905 regions with the 416 always has a greater link. Due to the congested environment and high price of housing and rent the trend of moving out of Toronto increased and this developed a strong link with the hinterlands. There are people who reside in Oshawa, Hamilton, and Mississauga, and come down to Toronto during the work week and return back to their suburban homes. This has led to certain cities in the GTA being called "bedroom communities".

The diversification of activities will not let Toronto down even at the peak of the recession. It covers everything from arable farming to dairy farming, manufacturing industries, service industries, finance and business, telecommunication and other communication networks, literature, pharmaceuticals, medical equipment, and tourism housing, has brought balanced growth to the Toronto economy. Depending on a single product, industry or a handful of them is very risky. As the old saying goes, it is never good to place all the eggs in one basket.

The city of Toronto is facing a couple of challenges and these have to be addressed sooner than later so as to avoid a volcanic eruption. The most recent challenge is that Toronto is believed to be on the top of the list to be attacked in revenge for Canadian support of the United States and the coalition forces fighting against terrorism .Though their agenda would have been very secret, Canada will change its stand in the near future and the target of the terrorists will be silenced. The change in the leadership of America in the long run will not change their agenda, but may slow it down.

The next challenges focus around the inadequate facilities and problems faced by low income earners that have not been resolved Their living conditions are not up to the standard of decent living in any urban city. I had witnessed this when I ran for office in the provincial government election. They do not have adequate subsidized rental accommodations, lack of day care facilities and in some cases the cost is not affordable, limited recreation facilities, fully protected areas where the crime rates are not going down and lack of counseling for parents and youth are some of the pressing concerns and my worry is that if these issues are not addressed in time with care it may lead to the beginning of unpleasant and destructive activities that will encourage unlawful activities, as an alternative. The third problem is the growing number of vehicles on the road causing traffic jams and accidents along with the increased cost of public transportation. I am very pleased that all three levels of government have agreed to extend the subway systems beyond the Toronto municipality. Medical care is always an issue for everyone in Canada and it consumes over forty percent of the budget. The waiting times are very long and many get frustrated and have lost confidence in the system. Though it is the responsibility of the provincial government not the municipality collaboration with GTA majors could be done to find ways and the means to pressure the provincial government. I am aware that most of these responsibilities have to be directed to the provincial and federal governments but the initiative and pressure have to come from the bottom at the grass root level and the municipal government cannot wash its hands of responsibility.

In spite of all these challenges Toronto is the safest and most tolerant city with an abundance of opportunities. Let us all work hard to elevate this city and in 25 years, let us throw a bicentennial celebration the likes of which have never been seen

CHAPTER NINETEEN

VISION FOR THE FUTURE OF CANADA

Over the years whenever I have visited foreign countries and had contact with friends, politicians, educators, dignitaries and others I have come to realize the unique position of Canada in the greater world community. There is no doubt that Canada is a very young nation blessed with an abundant variety of natural resources, a very clear vision for the future, a stable democratic system of government, a nation accepted as a non interfering country in terms of international affairs and recognized as a dignified nation that carries itself with integrity and respect. It should also be mentioned that this nation was built by immigrants from around the globe and this has garnered much respect on the world stage. In this fast changing modern world, we move at a steady pace accepting the fact that change is inevitable and is to be embraced. That being said, we must turn our focus to the future of this great country.

When I arrived in Canada over two decades ago some of my Canadian friends said that   the three main unpredictable things in Canada were the weather, work and women. Please do not misunderstand me neither my friends or myself believe in discrimination towards women; my friends who made this statement were only repeating something they had heard. Please note I had also heard some women say that men were unpredictable too. But today, the unpredictable variables are wider in range, deeper in nature and are a powerful force in moving this country forward. Globalization, the technological revolution, international politics, wars, the disintegration of nations, the formation of economic blocks, global warming, and changing climatic patterns, increasing crime and the dilution of family values will certainly have an impact on the future of Canada.

I would like to begin this discussion with the issue of human resources. The decline in the natural increase of the population is not an unusual trend when we are speaking about demographics. Historically speaking, when the Canadian economy got into the industrialized stage and a better standard of living was created, the cost living increased and the venue of having pleasure expanded from a mono source to multiple sources. As a result the usual customs of having children at an early age and many in number would not be preferred. This continues to be the case today. Whatever the support or encouragements given by the government and the influence of religious institutions on the issues of abortion, birth control, etc is not and will not have much impact as it used to. A good example is that most of the Quebecers have been practicing Catholics and the birth rate was very high for years but has gone down drastically over the course of time. Even new immigrants who come from cultural backgrounds that teach that the purpose of marriage is to have many children prefer to have fewer children, with the exception of some who happen to have baby girls and keep conceiving until they have a baby boy. I am very concerned that in a few decades, the death rate is going to supersede the birth rate. This will increase our dependency on foreign migration. There is also the possibility that with the development of more advanced technology that these new innovations could wind up replacing human beings to a certain extent.

Encouraging the migration of more skilled workers and investors is another potential source of fulfilling the shortage of manpower. The locations of the major source countries has shifted from the traditional European nations to selected Asian countries such as China, India and Pakistan where the population explosion has produced a surplus of highly educated people compared to their capital investment. The current rate of rapid economic growth in China and India will certainly and naturally slow down the natural rate of increase in the population and the accommodative capacity of most of the educated and skillful people will increase. This coupled with the standard of living along with the expansion of access to modern facilities will certainly slow down the migration rate. The scarcity of skilled and educated workers in European nations, the USA and Australia will compete with Canada in the international market for them. Canada has to become more attractive and stronger initiatives in bringing these talented people into Canada before those other competitive nations get them first are a must. The Canadian government realized the draw back of the current immigration system and took necessary steps in clearing the back log of over ninety thousand skilled worker applications. Mr. Jason Kenny, the Minister of Immigration made an announcement in the month of December, 2008 that all recently submitted applications and new applications will be processed within a year not the three to four years as it was in the past. The priority is given to certain groups of skilled workers whose services are required immediately. It is high time for an overhaul of the immigration policy so that future plans will work in conjunction with Canadian economic planning, the demographic distribution and social amenities

Without computer literacy anyone who knows the three R's (reading, writing and Arithmetic) will not be considered as literate anymore. In most cases of communication with the government and private sectors, the computer is going to be the most common and essential mode of communication. The new innovations and technological revolutions will bring the world closer and most of the transactions and communication will not go from person to person directly but to the technological devices and direct interaction between human beings will decrease.

Modern technology has penetrated the core of society, turning this vast world into a village. The extensive, broader and easier ways of operating these products from the high tech sector to day to day life has crossed political and ethnic boundaries and promotes the concepts associated with globalization. Human beings are going to share their gains and losses, knowledge and wisdom, will feel free to live anywhere, and marry the ones whom they like without the consideration of ethnicity, colour or linguistic barriers. Technology will also expand our notion of "community". I can give countless examples of the generosity of many Canadians. I shared in the sorrow and horror of the 26th December 2004 Tsunami in Southeast Asia and I was amazed at the generosity of Canadians in their contributions to the relief effort.

Our advanced technology allowed us to know about these disasters within hours of their occurrence. The earth quake in Kashmir, volcanic eruptions in the Philippines and the recent earthquake in central China also affirm our willingness to assist others. Even though we may not know these people directly we offer assistance as fellow members in the global family. In the future, this will continue even more.

Our billion dollar question centers on the economy; will the diversified and strong Canadian economy become stronger, remain the same or slow down in the near future? Canadians are very conservative in maintaining economic growth and keeping the strength steady. Consecutive Canadian governments even at the stage of economic slow down have focused on paying back the national debt by a sizeable amount compared to many other developed nations. The high quality working environment, moderate wages, standardized products, and the constant updating of technology and skills are keeping the Canadian economy stable. But Japanese companies that are established in Canada are not very pleased in terms of the employer – employee relationship and expect a friendlier atmosphere with more attention paid to the personal lives of the employees.

The effects of high level competition in the manufacturing of goods in international trade with Canada some how woke up Ontario and Quebec. Since America is the single major buyer of these products, Canada has to dance according to the tune of American economic conditions and policies. Countries like China export more consumer goods and eventually penetrate into the high tech product sector and machinery which in turn becomes a challenge to us. Having better product lines would not catch a better market and we have to explore new markets with new visions. Alberta suddenly became a rich province by generating revenue mainly from oil, a single commodity. Even though Alberta has the second largest oil deposit in the country, it will be exhausted in a period of time and there may be a risk of reduction in the importance of oil by alternative sources of energy. Newfoundland recently discovered oil and even though it has not reached a high level of production, it is always risky to have all the eggs in the same basket. The North though it is not densely populated is rich in minerals. But unresolved border disputes with the U.S, Russia and Denmark will certainly receive better attention from the federal government and the rest of Canada. The regional barriers among the provinces are not appreciated by many and preferred by some. Eventually these barriers will be relaxed and trade between the provinces will flourish.

The seeds of regional autonomy are like the winter wheat buried in the ground in fall, lie dormant during the winter and germinate when spring arrives. The interest in having regional autonomy and turn away from confederation did not originate in Quebec. Before the formation of the federation there were groups who actively advocated for regional autonomy for Quebec in Nova Scotia. The Maritime region elected 19 anti-confederation members of parliament in the first election in 1867. More recently in the 1990's some of the prominent members of Parliament stated that if Quebec left Canada, they would try to join the United States of America. The current population of Atlantic Canada is closer to the size of Ontario. The main contribution of the Atlantic Provinces is not only the sweet fish, but also the wonderful brain power and they are proud of saying that their major export is the brain.

Alberta in the Wild West all of a sudden became a fabulously rich province in Canada and the wild wind that blows in the west over central Canada to Ontario and Quebec dominates and holds undue power in Canadian politics and other public affairs. This has been fading and relations are becoming closer and more cordial in general, but some Alberta citizens began to think that it would have been much better getting out from confederation and becoming an independent nation. Of course the Quebec issue is not dead and buried. Unless the federal government makes some changes in the constitution, and adds amendments regarding unilateral decisions by provinces to leave the confederation this will be inactive bacteria in the winter and summer and get activated in the fall and spring. The resulting flu will weaken the federal system of government. The time is the right to develop some fundamental changes to the constitution of Canada with modifications, eliminations and additions of certain sections aimed at the best interests of a future Canada.

The relationship between the provinces as a whole with the federal government in maintaining, renovating and expanding the Canadian socio-economic and ethnic fabric should keep best interest of the nation intact. In terms of sharing the responsibilities and the wealth; instead of the federal government transferring certain responsibilities without transferring adequate funds it is like a game of musical chairs. The provincial governments play a similar game. In the past when federal governments had surplus budgets many of the provinces had deficits or struggled to have a balanced budget by reducing services and increasing direct and indirect taxes. I do agree in certain cases that the provincial government would have better a budget if they managed their financial and economic plans well and not pass the entire blame on the federal government. The relationship is not always centered on blaming each other and expecting a larger share from the national cake or bargain in getting more power from the federal government. Of course the mandate and the interest of the provincial agenda supersede the national interest at times. When I contested in the provincial election of 2007 I came across in sharing and drawing a line between federal and provincial demarcations.

Many families are very worried about getting good quality education for their children. Alongside this issue are concerns about receiving better and more timely health care services on a single tier system, affordable housing, better and cheaper transportation facilities, law and order, better relations with multi ethnic groups, lower taxes, better social amenities , broader child care services, and employment security.

There are numerous criticisms about the current system of education and its implementation however, when compared with many other developed nations it is one of the leaders. This means that in the fast changing and challenging socio-economic and technological world, Canada has to act and accommodate these changes quickly. Lower school enrolment due to the lower birth rate will allow for more allocation of money for investing in the modernization of the school system. The allocation of more capital in the field of educational research will lead to efficient future workers in this country. Teaching is a noble profession and more allocation of money alone will not improve the system, rather parents, children, communities, teachers, governments and the administrators should work together to improve the quality of education. Our schools should act as community centers where everyone can participate.

The challenge that our health care system has in almost all of the provinces is the rising cost of providing free health care services. Unlike the USA where patients have to pay for healthcare, it consumes almost one third or more of the provincial budgets and leaves little money for the rest of the expenditures. Furthermore, many of us do not want to have a two tier system in which the rich will have better treatment the rest will not have equal access. Medical treatment should be prioritized based on the seriousness of the illness and urgency needed for treatment not according to the sum of the payment. It is true that those who can afford to do so seek for treatment in private clinics and this allows the rest to have more shares of the health care service and lower periods of waiting. But the adverse effects of the two tier system are high. The way things are moving it appears that soon, the two tier system will be introduced. The lack of doctors is another problem in many provinces. In Ontario, one of the most highly developed provinces having over thirteen million in population, over a million Ontarians are without a family doctor and they do not have an electronic file. Wherever these people go for treatment, the doctor would not be able to treat them well without having the current medical history of the patient. Hopefully most of the provinces will have electronic filing systems in place in the near future. Canadian drugs have been in very high demand in the United State due to the fact that the cost is cheaper and it creates a shortage and other inconveniences to Canadians. Let the States buy more Canadian beef, softwood lumber, and oil sand products instead of more drugs.

The expansion of public transportation facilities and higher volumes of usage will reduce air pollution, accidents on the road and traffic jams. Most of the roads have to be repaired and maintained and new roads, railways and subway lines have to be constructed. Cheap vehicles that have been produced in India and China may encourage more people to buy cars, but this endangers Canadian jobs. The cost of oil and gas is also a factor. Unless the price goes down, more people will leave their cars behind and switch to public transit.

Having a crime free environment is only a dream, but reducing crime is required in Canada and when we compare the crime rates, in many places it is rising but compared with similar developed nations and its cosmopolitan cites in the would, our crime rate is much lower and we appreciate the officers who have been doing their job well. Since I have been serving as one of the members of the consultation committee for the South and West Divisions of the Toronto Police service, I have experienced the need for the community to work more closely with the police and take more preventive measures. Still the crime rate has to go down and every one of us should be confident that they are safe in the parking lot, on the streets and in their homes. It would be much better if many young people from multiple ethnic groups chose to become police officers, so that its services will easily penetrate into various group of people in big cities like Toronto, Hamilton, Ottawa, Montreal, Edmonton, Vancouver, in particular.

Canadian participation in peace keeping and contributing in humanitarian operations is what the world expects from us, and the world expects more in this regard. Although Canada does not gain much, it sacrifices a lot in terms of man power and wealth at the cost of the tax payers and this has to be recognized. Though Canadians would not worry about it, its selfless service to humanity and world peace is well appreciated and should continue more in the future. It keeps the Canadian image high and positive. The Canadian flag can be seen all around troubled waters and no nation should enter into our waters illegally and make it troubled. Canadians have never hesitated in making sacrifices to promote international peace around the world and we should be proud.

Every Canadian should put the interest of the nation first, no matter which region you come from, what ethnicity you belong to, or which political party you are attached to. These things do not matter. What does matter is that we are all Canadians. Our patriotic feelings and actions are required to make the future brighter, richer, cordial and better.

The destiny of Canada is not going to remain as it is today. For better or for worse, the ball is in your court.

REFERENCE

1) Frederick H. Armstrong; City in the Making

2) Rudyard Griffiths Canada in 2020

3) Darrell Bricker & John Wright What Canadians think

4) Peter A. Baskerville Ontario Image Identity and power

5) Robert R. Bonis A history of Scarborough

6) Chairs Cotter Toronto between wars

7) Joson Mcbride & Alana Wilcox UTOPIA Towards a new Toronto

8) G. Gagnon Quebec

9) Michael D. Behiels Quebec since 1800

10) Stephen G. Tomblim & T= Charles S. Colgan Regionalism in a Global society

11) William C. Wonders Canada's changing north

12) Knowlton Nasa Visions of Canada

13) Olive Patricia Dickson Canada's First nations.

14) Mario Pei The story of language

15) David Matas, Llana Simon Closing the Doors

16) Peter Stalker The work of strangers

17) Valerie Knowles Strangers at our gates

18) James Bickerton & Alain G. Gagnon Canadian Politics

19) Mel Hurtig The vanishing Country

20) William Johnson Stephen Harper

21) Michael Bliss Right Honourable men

22) Andre Pratte Quebec federalists speak up for change

INDEX

A

Abortion   27, 174
Acceptance Ratio   7
Accommodative immigration policy
   97
Accumulated bills   53
Additional language   51
Afrikaans   49
Afro-centric   40
Aids   31
The American revolution   2, 9, 95,
   168
Amharic   31
Amnesty international   25
Ancestral   ix-x, 1-2, 46, 115, 141
Ancestral homeland   2, 141
Ancestral language   46
Ancient roots   46
Anglo-Indians   67
Anti-Americanism   14
Apartheid   92, 122, 130
Arabic numerical system   46
Arable   19, 59, 97, 117, 152, 169
Archaeological   55, 113
arm's-length   10
Armed conflict   7, 45, 59, 148
Article   30, 37, 63, 87, 89, 97, 111,
   153, 166
Asia   viii-ix, 4, 18-19, 24, 26, 49,
   55, 73, 105, 112, 128-9, 132,
   136, 147, 152, 175

Assimilated   60, 102
Astronaut   17
Asylum   25-6, 28, 31, 74, 81-2
Asylum seekers and refugees   74
Atmosphere   36, 132, 168, 176
Attained   5-6, 21
Australia   25-6, 49, 68, 82, 147,
   174
Austrians   60, 102
Authoritarian   40
authorities   4, 24, 31, 39, 102, 127

B

Baby boomers   8, 47, 64, 72, 109,
   158
Barack Obama   92, 101, 127, 141
Basic right   57, 118
Bilingual nation   4
Bilingualism   45-7, 50-1
Birds   17, 72, 137-8, 152
Birth rate   21, 37, 55-8, 64, 93,
   109, 115, 131, 158, 174, 178
Blamed for the economic hardship
   66
Blessing   54, 68, 90, 155, 165, 167
Bloc Quebecois   3, 90
Boat people   73, 84
Bondar, Roberta   17
Borders   6, 9, 17
Bosnia   28, 65
Bottom line   14, 46, 70

LaVergne, TN USA
16 April 2010
179550LV00003B/255/P